CW01667513

One Way To Rock
The Ultimate Collection of Fan Stories
Sammy Hagar

Created by Shellie Chambers-Keylon

Edited by Shelley Shepherd-Klaner

Shellie Keylon shelliekeylon13@gmail.com

Paperback ISBN: 979-8-9869713-0-8
eBook ISBN: 979-8-9869713-1-5

Printed in the United States of America

Introduction

This book began as a dream by Shellie Keylon to allow Sammy Hagar fans, aka Redheads, to share their stories. Some of the stories are long and heart-wrenching; others are just musings of what Sammy has meant to his fans through the years. Stories are edited for space and clarity. None of the submitted stories were written by professional writers. In steps Shelley Shepherd-Klaner, who is a professional writer and has written many stories about Sammy Hagar, Chickenfoot, Montrose and other bands to edit and compile the book. Tommie Gerbic provided illustration work. We hope this book brings amusement to Sammy Hagar fans and friends and to Sammy himself. It was started as a gift for Sammy for his 75th birthday. Happy birthday Sammy. All proceeds will cover costs and will be donated to Sammy's favorite charities.

A birthday tribute from Velma Hagar

My little Bro Sam out did them all..

As he picked and sang and heard his call…

He started at the bottom, a family without class,

They said he'd never make it, he'd fall on his ass..

Everyone said cut your hair and go to work

But he always knew around the corner success did lurk.

He struggled as he sang his way to the top

With charisma and a style that included his mop.

Born with hair that was a wild mass of frizz

It was blond and massive and uniquely his.

He chose to wear RED and screamed his way to the top

Running and jumping while shaking his mop.

He partied like a beach bum and stuck with his style

Treating his fans like family all of the while.

Everyone loved him as they flocked to his show

Bound and determined where he went; they would go.

The Redheads were formed and always stuck together

Forming an amazing friendship through all kinds of weather.

They supported each other and adored their King,

And At the Cabo Wabo they would dance and sing.

They knew all of his songs and sang them out loud

As their guy in RED always made them proud.

The years have flown by but Sam never quit

What he has to give, he gives every bit.

He has remained Young and his hair is still a mass

And finally the name Hagar has tremendous class.

His sister is proud and loves him from her heart and she always has right from the start.

Happy Birthday baby Bro.

Lauren Vercruysse

I was Living in the San Francisco Bay the first time I saw Sammy in concert. It was 1975, (16 years old), at the San Jose Center for the Performing Arts. Sammy was the opening band for Earthquake, and Journey was the headliner, sans Steve Perry. Nine on a Ten scale album had just been released. The local radio station, KSJO, was always playing Young Girl Blues, the first airplay song of Sammy's solo career.

Moving back to Michigan, the next concert for me was Toledo Speedway Jam in 1980, (200,000 fans), and 350 kegs of beer. Making my way to the front, I remember him playing Bad Motor Scooter. He sat on the edge of the stage with that slide Guitar, stood up, and threw it to a roadie all the way across the stage, nearly dropping it!

I was fortunate enough to see Sammy four more times. Once at Pine Knob outdoor amphitheater in the Detroit area, twice in Lansing Michigan, (2008, 2010), at Common Ground RiverFront. Those were the shows with the Wabaritos; girls on stage serving Sammy's Waborita drink and fans all across the back of the stage on the risers.

The show in Detroit with Chickenfoot was awesome. It was Sammy's Super group. A different side of him, but the way they all gelled as one great group was amazing. 2014 was the tour with The Circle. That concert started another era. That night the set included a Chicken Foot song and was dropped after the next show. It was amazing seeing Michael, Vic, and Jason playing 40 Years of Sammy's music, (Montrose, Chickenfoot, and Led Zeppelin).

I've been going to Cabo since 2018 and always spend time at the Cabo Wabo Cantina. I have not seen Sammy in the club yet. He's been in town or I have missed seeing him by a couple of days, (That's what dreams are made of). I have tickets this August at Pine Knob music theater again to the Crazy Times tour and am so excited to be in Cabo this year for the Birthday Bash. Although many of you have met and have been fortunate enough to get pictures with him or autographed items, many of us are still just having (Dreams) or (High Hopes) where (Eagle's Fly), to have a meet and greet.

Locks of Love
By Adam Kanning

Happy birthday to the man who is one of the greatest inspirations in my life — Sammy Hagar. How many times in life do we get to experience the true beauty of music? For me, it's every single day I had the fortune of growing up in a family that lives and breathes music. Growing up on the family farm, I was surrounded by music. My grandfather, aunts, uncles, and father were all musicians. Every weekend we heard the sounds of guitars, banjos, fiddles, ukuleles, and a piano.

In 1973 I bought my first guitar at a rummage sale. I literally played until my fingers bled. Although my father played country music, I took an immediate liking to rock and roll. In 1978, I bought a Van Halen record. The bar for guitar had been raised. Although I wasn't interested in imitating Eddie, I did begin to realize music has no limitations. I continued to hone my guitar playing and working on my pipes. I played in several bands. But in 1986, I was given another lesson in what music really is. Van Halen released its newest record *5150*. A new member had emerged; Sammy Hagar. His energy entered my life.

In 1988 my world changed. The place was Denver, Col.. The event was Monsters of Rock. I finally had the opportunity to hear hours of rock and roll, but more than that, I finally was able to see the band in action. Sammy's stage presence filled my soul. For the first time in my life, I felt the "give and take" that music has to offer. As I fought through the crowd to get as close as I could, a feeling of "oneness" overcame me. The crowd was feeding off your energy, and you were feeding it back. I was in complete awe.

In 1999 Sammy was a guest on the *Tonight Show*. I watched in horror, as Sammy had his long hair cut and donated it to Locks of Love. I learned the lesson of giving. In 2000, I cut my hair and donated it to Locks of Love. Later I did it again.

In early 2012, my father began losing his battle with cancer. In his last weeks, I would bring my guitar to the hospital and play. Every day he would request a song, usually Sammy's song *Eagles Fly*. He was not only a guitar player, but also a pilot. He loved the connection this tune brought to him, and I loved I could be the beacon to bring them together before he passed away.

By Jeff Forrester

Saw Sammy at Monsters of Rock at the Liberty Bowl in Memphis, Tenn. in 1988, when he was in Van Halen. It was an all-day concert and was the best ever. I have never met Sammy. In 1984 I was stationed in Guam when I was in the U.S. Air Force. I saw Montrose there without Sammy, It was a good show. Then I saw him and Vic Johnson at the Allstar Race at the Texas Motor Speedway. I've been following his music since Montrose. Just such a fan. Next stop Cabo.

By Felicia Urioste

I've been seeing Sammy in concert since the 80's. I love his music and the way he loves his fans. During one of his concerts in St Louis, I was at his 'Sammy Catina' and I met some people who are still friends 15 years later. We have gone on trips to Tahoe to see Sammy where I got to meet so many more Redheads that have become friends. I even met Sammy's son at the Ratrunner. My son met Sammy when he was 5 years old, and now he 19.

I have had the opportunity to meet Sammy several times. I've been to Vegas, Tahoe, Cabo, and of course, St. Louis where I live. Cabo is my favorite trip where all of the friends I have made came together for a good time. I love listening to his music as it makes me feel happy even when things aren't going well in life.

What is very impressive is how down-to-earth and generous he is. He donates his time and money to help others in need. Besides loving Sammy and his music, I love the way he has brought me so many great memories and friendships that I will always remember. Happy 75 th Birthday Sammy

I Can't Stop Loving You

By Teri Johnson

I have been a fan of Sammy's music since the Montrose days. His music always put a smile on my face. Then I read his book *Red My Uncensored Life in Rock* and became a fan of Sam, the man. The first time I saw him live was with Chickenfoot in 2009, the first Chickenfoot show of the tour in Seattle, at El Corazón. We started going to Cabo and have had the chance of seeing and talking to him there. He is a gem whose light shines on and touches everyone he meets. We are all put on this earth for a purpose and he definitely followed the right path for his journey. The passion he has for his music and sharing that with all of us is an amazing gift of love. My most memorable moment to date would be October 2021 at the Cabo Wabo Cantina in CSL. I was fortunate to be an "upfront fanatic" and as he was singing *I Can't Stop Loving* You he reached down and held my hand, singing to me, then put his microphone down in front of me as I was singing along with him. At the end of the show, he handed me his bottle of Santo Tequila to finish off. For so many years he has touched hearts and put smiles on so many faces. He Rocks in so many ways

Green Eggs and Ham

By Mary Connell Healey

I have so many stories it's hard to choose which to share. I don't remember exact dates because I have been to more shows with my husband than I can even count in the past 30 years.

We were going to see the 'Sam I Am' tour, near Buffalo. A week before the show, the theme hit me and all I could think of was one of my son's favorite bedtime stories. He's about 23 now and he was about four at the time, so that's about as close as a time reference as I have. I mentioned the coincidence of our son's favorite *Green Eggs and Ham* story to my husband, and he shrugged it off. I somehow managed the day of the show, to sneak my son's book out of the house. It had been through two children so there were some crayon drawings inside and it was well loved, especially by my son.

We went to that particular show with my former neighbor, my brother-in-law and a group of his friends. We partied and "pre-showed" in the parking lot for hours meeting more Sammy fans, feeling like we were part of a new community. So many kind people, each cranking their favorite Sammy songs, fold-up chairs everywhere and plenty of drinks to go around. Frisbies being thrown with footballs and spontaneous beach balls.

As we were getting ready to head into the show, front row as usual, I changed and put the book in my purse that I was taking in with me. My husband noticed the book and just gave me a "you have to be kidding me" look. He wasn't surprised as I always do "quirky" things but didn't seem all that thrilled either.

Once in the venue, I sat up my location in front of Mikey's side as I did each and every show. The show started with a bang, and we were all having a blast when Mikey seemed to recognize me and I received a hug from him on stage. I also smuggled in some shot bottles of Jack Daniels, which Mikey and I enjoyed.

As the show went on and Sammy started to do some signing of shirts and whatever was thrown at him, my neighbor got his shirt signed and was so excited. I decided it was now or never and I reached into my bag and grabbed the book. My husband is much taller and has a better reach so he figured he would have better luck getting Sammy's attention and he took it and held it high.

Sammy had his *Cat in the Hat* hat on and was just heading into *I Can't Drive 55,* when he noticed the book. He took it right from my husband's hand and proceeded to sit on the stage and act as if he was reading it. The band just kept playing the intro to the song because Sammy was in no rush with this incredibly special moment for a fan. He signed the front cover, but quickly noticed it would come right off so he opened the front cover and signed it

He came right back to my husband and handed it to him and it was no longer the "damn my wife is weird" look.... It was my wife is a friggin genius look.

Not only did Sammy fans catch this on video and post it online but when Sammy's photo book came out, there was an amazing shot of him sitting on stage with my book in his hands. The next show we attended we brought our photo book and Sammy seemed to remember that we were the *Green Eggs and Ham* book couple and he gladly signed our photo book cover and shook our hands.

I could literally write my own book with all of the amazing memories I have from all of the shows I've attended with my husband. The first autograph we received when Eddie wore my husband's shirt on his head for an entire song before Sammy signed it and when my husband got it back, held it tight to this chest with tears running down his cheeks.

All of the shots of Jack Daniels I've been honored to do with Mikey, being busted by Sammy who stopped the show and lectured Mikey and I that we should be drinking his tequila, letting Mikey finish his guitar solo, while he went off stage and had a drink made just for me.

The last show we attended was in 2021 in Vegas and I let my husband have his dream night and meet the entire band. Memories I know he will hold close forever, and I will never regret giving him.

These stories are all bittersweet, however as by the time this book is published, I will have attended my last show. My body has decided it has taken as much as it can, and I am hoping to get to thank Sammy, Mikey, Vic and Jason for all the amazing memories I will always have in my heart thanks to them.

"Rockstars" have a stigma that in no way applies to Sammy. He truly loves what he does and I feel so honored that I've been allowed to be a part of this wonderful group of people we've met throughout the year who are now considered friends. Thank you for the amazing shows but most of all, for all the amazing memories Sammy.

I Gave My First Love the Finger

By Catherine Hartshorn

It's hard to even tell when life began and when Sammy began.

I dated a guy in high school (my first love) and in 1984 he broke my heart. I listened to *I'll Fall In Love Again* about a billion times. It gave me strength to give him the finger.

I purchased my first car in 1984. It was a red and white Mustang that I named the "Red Rocker". The personalized plates read "REDROKR". Nothing but Sammy playing most of the time. I have a picture of it with me beside it with my feathered hair. Everyone on the strip ,while cruising knew the Red Rocker "and" the REDROKR". My cousin had a stereo store and I had the baddest system in the world. When I sold the REDROKR, it was to a gal who was deaf. She said she could "feel" the music in the car.

Later, when I was in college I had the *HSAS* album. I am not sure if it really ever took off — but Sammy sang the best cover of *Whiter Shade of Pale* - EVER. I turned some friends onto it at the time and to this day I ask just about everyone who tells me they are a Sammy fan about that song. I play it for them on my stereo or my phone. They just love it.

After college, the album mysteriously disappeared. It took me years to find one. My late husband and I were I a record store in Portland Ore. and found it. I then purchased two just in case.

In 2012, I went to Cabo Wabo in Cabo San Lucas for the first time. I purchased Sammy's book and (and a bottle of his tequila of course). My favorite drink was the "Red Rocker". When I went to the Cabo Wabo in Las Vegas years later, it had been discontinued - however, I had a picture of the actual menu on my phone from my first visit to Cabo and they were able to recreate it. The Cabo Wabo Reposado with the lime and cranberry juice with a hint of Amaretto - just sings in your mouth

Well, I cannot say enough about the impact that Sammy has had on my life during the last 40 some years. It's been an honor and a privilege to be on the planet at the same time as Sammy.

Musings

By Dale Calantoni-Baker

I have been a fan since well before VH! One of Sammy's early albums hooked me I never had a chance to see him live, but he did perform one song on stage with my favorite band Journey I'm not sure if the year was 2003 or 2005. About four years ago, I made a stained-glass piece for Sammy. My dream is to meet him and give him the gift. He is an awesome singer and has worked with many of my other favorite musicians. Keep Rockin' Red Rocker.

Sammy Love Through the Generations

By Bill Maio

Let me take you back, back in time —

Okay I know Huey Lewis, but hey we have to start this some way. It was the summer of 1984, I was in seventh grade, a simple good child from a Chicago blue-collar family. Enjoying life like many of us from the '80s: playing sports, bike-riding with friends, hanging out at the park, playing kick-the-can, drinking from garden hoses, and making sure we were home when the streetlights were on.

Listening to top 40 on the radio, something was missing, *That only one way to rock*. Previously that year, I was introduced to Van Halen. A friend says: "You like VH and Ozzy. You need to check out Sammy Hagar." I went to the local record store and purchased Sammy Hagar's *VOA*. After listening to the album, I was addicted. The lyrics, the guitar riffs, the vocals. I became a huge fan, bought every record; even back to the Montrose days.

Sammy encouraged me to learn to play guitar. The day he joined Van Halen, I was amazed, since I was a huge Van Halen fan already. It truly was the best of both worlds. Sammy brought a whole new dimension to an already amazing group — that missing piece of added guitar harmony and vocal brilliance. He was the perfect fit for a perfect time. Eighties hair bands, Hagar and Van Halen, more specifically opened my eyes to more music excitement. Those albums inspired me to look into bands like Motley Crue and Skid Row. It created a needed escape from the normal teenager problems. I could find solace slapping on head phones, dropping a cassette in my Walkman, or listening to my record player and drifting away into the music and lyrics. All this really ignited my passion for music and guitar.

Now being an avid concert goer, I've seen Sammy with Van Halen, solo, and with The Circle. I've seen him more than 20 times so far, and cannot wait for the next show. That's saying a lot being that I have seen some 490 bands live. This love for music and guitar, which was started by Mr. Hagar has only grown to extreme infatuation. My music listening lifestyle has grown to all genres of music.

Seeing Sammy in concert the first time after his departure from Van Halen with him and Mike Anthony was another new turning point. Watching The chemistry between them is amazing. Their music turns any day around. So many of Sammy's songs truly have deep meaning to me and things I experienced through my 50-year lifetime. Sammy's lyrics and songs help me get through my darkest of days and my happiest of times.

When you see Sammy on stage you NEVER see a frown or a musician just and working, it's something he enjoys in his heart, and it shows. Passing my musical knowledge down to my children, who are now also fans of every genre was important to me. They attend many concerts with me as well as they were raise to enjoy the art of music and get lost in the songs. Sammy is true music genius. I even traveled to Cabo in hopes to catch a glimpse of the man for an impromptu show. Unfortunately, I was not that lucky. I avidly try to get to be one of the lucky ones to attend birthday shows in Cabo, but so far have been unsuccessful. One day I hope that will come true. One of the most fun concerts was when I was stage side at Festival of the Lakes in Hammond Indiana. Sammy is an inspiration for many — old and young.

Musings

By Michelle Pepper

I've been a fan since the Montrose days. I loved Sammy's passion and dedication towards his fans. Someone invited me to attend a Rum Party at Club Vinyl in the Hard Rock/Vegas. It was the grand opening for Club Vinyl and Sammy's Beach Bar Rum debut. I got on the guest list and had a blast. I never miss a show. My license plate says it all...REDROQR Keep playing for us, we love you.

By Glenn Nicholson

In 1992, I saw you guys in a Hartford, Conn. concert. It was the night before my real analysis exam at Eastern CT State University. I had a little guilt that I should be studying instead of rocking it out with you guys. Sometimes in life you just say, "Fuck it." I still managed to get a B on the exam. Your show was incredible. I love you guys and definitely missing Eddie.

Me and my baby

By Maria P. Apostolopoulos-Yarrington

Hello Baby!

(I'm) not quite sure when I fell in love with Sammy's music and melodic voice. His voice is so captivating, soothing, and, for lack of a better word — kick ass.

I think I first heard either *Can't Get Loose* and/or *Heavy Metal* in the early '80s, I was hooked. It moved me, and I felt that Sammy was speaking directly to me. I feel like there is a song for everything, like Sammy's music is literally the soundtrack to my life. It has helped me through dark times and good times.

When I was 22-years-old, I graduated college, got a "real" job, and bought my first car: a Chevy Cavalier V24 Coupe. I was on top of the world. While driving off the lot, the Loop was playing *Top of the World* and I felt like I was right there.

Then, at 32 and only married for a few years, I was diagnosed with breast cancer. It was an early stage, but very aggressive. I had to undergo four cycles of chemo. I would go in once every three weeks, if memory serves me, for a four-hour drip of some stuff that looked like rat poison. After all that chemo, I had to endure radiation treatment. I drove myself every day for eight weeks for treatment. They literally had to strap my hands and legs down to tattoo the location the radiation would have to go because I was kicking and screaming since it hurt like hell. I literally felt like I could not get loose, but I had to fight like hell to keep my spirits up and not fall into the abyss. Watching my hair fall out, having to shave it, and then having to get a wig was just devastating; especially since, at that time I was in technology sales and I was the only female on an all-male team. It should not matter, but it does. My husband, the wonderful man that he is, made me a mix-tape of Sammy's solo and Van Halen music a, along with Def Leppard, Rush, Journey, and other great rock bands that I blasted on my Walkman, which I still have to this day. It was my escape from what I was going through. Sammy's music got me through it all. I literally had to find my inner-bitch, strap my proverbial balls on, and fight like hell.

Flash forward to when I was finally able to get pregnant; found out I was pregnant; the first thing I did was grab those CD's and Walkman and strapped the headphones to my belly to let my child hear what great music was. Giving birth was rough for me. I was 35 and I had a difficult delivery. Then, "Hello, Baby" my beautiful little girl was born. I had the best of both worlds. I had my health and a beautiful daughter, whom I named Paige. My daughter is now 18 and left for college. She is a Sammy/Van Halen fan and loved the bands I grew up with.

Kids her age often think she is weird because she does not like rap and hip hop. She is a rocker, a Red Rocker, like her mom. She tells her peers she has an "old soul" when it comes to music and greatly prefers the complexity and artistry of rock music to modern music.

I am proud to say that I am 22 years in remission, and both my daughter and I have a special bond of loving the same music. Sammy's music. THERE IS ONLY ONE WAY TO ROCK, AND THAT IS THE RED ROCKER WAY!

I Wet My Britches

By Jennifer Burkhalter

My first ever Cabo BDB experience was October 2009. I, like everyone else, was earning my stripes as a true Redhead by "sleeping" on the street in Cabo outside the Cantina. Actually I hardly slept. It was a 24-hour Redhead party. It was so much fun and I met so many friends.

I saw Sammy several times in the states, but this was EXTRA special. When he arrived in his van with a security team, who kept us safe all night and attempted to escort Sammy safely into the entrance, he stopped and took the time to connect with his half-drunk, sleepy, sweaty fans. It was at that point that I KNEW that THIS was the Next-Level Redhead experience. Although we had seen Sammy several times and were lucky enough to be on the risers in Ohio, the Cabo experience was amazing.

One of my adventures was with Redhead Jill, who taught me the Cabo ins and outs. We had dinner before the concert and then we ran because we needed to get out the door to be upfront and center at Cabo Wabo. I watched in awe as Bro, then Vic, Mona, and finally. THE REDROCKER himself came downstairs to the stage (I think I wet my britches at that point. But, I didn't care at all, I after all was a Texas girl.After the show I got autographs and photos. Sammy is the most giving, happy superstar, who loves his fans, bringing joy and peace in the world.

You're in the Army Now

By Herb Patton

I've been a huge fan of Sammy for a long time. My favorite concert was the first time I saw Sammy at the Summit in Houston and the concert shirt is still hanging in my closet.

When Sammy joined VanHalen, I couldn't have been happier. I played the cassette that was worn out before I got the CD. I was counting the days until the Van Halen 5150 tour. But I didn't get to go as I had to report to basic training for the U.S. Army. I tried to get my recruiter to change it, but the contract was signed.

That didn't stop me from attending 10 more shows and someday I will see Sammy in Cabo. I entered the contest for your Birthday Bash, and I was one of the winners, but couldn't go. I was in Dallas for a free show along with like 20,000 other fans. I drove from Oklahoma to the show soon as I heard it on the radio that morning.

One of many memories was waiting to see Van Halen on the Balance tour in Austin. We were sitting in a line of cars and a group of limos being escorted by police passed us by and when Sammy's got next to us he stuck out his head and waved to fans in line. I was shocked I was so close to the singer of my favorite band.

Sammy is dedicated to his fans and I have witnessed him sign many autographs. I have to thank him as the world of Rock 'n Roll exists because of people like him .

Happy 75th birthday Sammy. Hope to be in Cabo in 2023.

Musings

By John Dettore

I was living in Vegas 1999. The KOMP radio station had a contest for a meet and greet before Sammy's show. I was getting ready for work; 7:55 a.m. I remember it like it was yesterday. I was the right caller, and won the contest. Three days before my birthday, on the July 6 and I got to meet Sammy. He was the nicest, coolest guy. I think five people wont meet him.. Next, Sammy says: "I got something special for one of you guys." He had put our names in a hat and picked a name to win one of his guitars. I didn't win, but I was still excited that I got to meet the Red Rocker — my favorite rocker. Went to the show. I've seen Sammy live 25 times. Every show was amazing. I've never gotten to see him front row. That would surpass any bucket list. Keep on rocking, Sammy, and I love my baby's poundcake. Thank you for all the years of the greatest tunes on earth. Hope to see you in Connecticut soon.

Jumping for Sammy in my Nike Air Hurraches

By Jamie McCullagh

My obsession started in the '80s here in Australia when I first heard Van Halen cranking on the local radio stations. It wasn't until much later I discovered Sammy's back catalogue of work, which is equally impressive.

My friends James Guy, Gary Woodward and Andrew Gooding were all huddled around the TV at James' parents house as he had received the latest video release, *Live Without a Net*. We had to watch at their house as they were the only ones on the street with a dual format VHS player capable of playing it. I remember the excitement and awe of watching Sammy live for the first time, I was hooked from this moment on, which turned to obsession. I used to strut around in my Nike Air Huaraches, the exact same ones that Sammy wore on stage.

Back in 1998, Sammy finally toured down under. I saw Sammy in person for the first time at the Palais in St Kilda, Melbourne, along with James and Gary. We were in the front row, up-front fanatics if you like. Ever since that night I had this burning desire to see Sammy again. I joined FaceBook pages, followed the Redrocker.com website and eventually stumbled across Club 1013, all the while my passion was growing.

In 2018 I entered the lottery and won tickets to the Birthday Bash and low and behold so did James. Since we were coming from Australia we arranged a road trip taking us from New Orleans and Hollywood and to Vegas

That's where the party began as I met so many Redheads, full of passion for Sammy. I was offered a dinner ticket but I had to find a tall guy with a Hawaiian shirt and a shark tooth around his neck to get the tickets — not so easy in downtown Cabo.

So here we are in 2022, post -ovid and ready to travel. I put my name in the lottery and once again was lucky to win tickets. I am looking forward to catching up with the Mayor of Cabo Bryan Shaul who has helped every step of the way with accommodations and advice. Also I am excited to be part of this book for your birthday and I contributed to the auction to help fund it. Sammy, thank you for all the great memories.

Musings

By Bruce Meyers

I grew up in the country with little to no exposure to rock music. At the age of 18, (1979), I went to my first concert in Boston. Some guy I had never heard of named Sammy Hagar was the opening act. I left the show a Hagar fan. I have made it to every Sammy tour except the last Chickenfoot tour. I saw Sammy on my 50th birthday at the House of Blues in New Orleans. I've been to Cabo, as well as on the first Cabo cruise. I saw two recent shows at The Strat in Vegas.

I Turned up the Music

By Janett Wyatt

In 1982 I was introduced to Sammy's music by David McConnell, (see page xx), who had been listening and loving the tunes since he was in high school. When I was 21 in 1983, we attended The Three Lock Box Tour concert at the Orange Pavilion in San Bernardino.

That concert was a great experience and the beginning of my obsession. I can still picture Bill Church playing bass guitar to *Remember The Heroes...* it was so empowering. Although *Your Love Is Driving Me Crazy* was probably my favorite song.

In the past few years I rekindled my passion for concerts, starting off with attending the Birthday Bash in Huntington Beach. I bought tickets for the second bash and was disappointed when it was cancelled, but was able to attend the first day of the residency at the Strat in 2021. The decorations made you feel like you were in Cabo. My dream is to actually get to Cabo and meet Sammy in person.

I moved from California to Arizona, allowing me to see shows at Harrah's and the E-Center (although it was cut short due to the crazy weather) and Phoenix.

Many years I was unable to attend concerts but my record library includes all your albums in one format or another; vintage vinyl, cassettes, CDs, videos and electronically, with some of the albums in multiple formats.

My appreciation for Sammy extends to his down-to-earth humanitarian values. From always giving back and showing appreciation to the fans to fellow artists such as at Tribute to Eddie Money at the Saban Theatre in Beverly Hills.

I credit Sammy for touching my life in so many ways from his music, concerts and memories and inspiration provided. His music and the meaning behind the songs have gotten me through some very rough patches in my life and helped me to go on. Thankfully, with the rough patches behind me, I can again enjoy attending concerts and turning up the music..

Photo Courtesy of Chris Massey

The Soundtrack of my Life

By Brett Carroll

My introduction to Sammy was *5150,* back in 1986.I hadn't heard much about VH previously, only *Jump*, and Sammy's popularity in Australia wasn't very big neither. I just remember hearing Dave had left, and Sammy joined. To be honest, when I first heard *Why Can't This be Love*, it did nothing for me, but a few months later everything changed when a friend played me *5150*. From then on, I was obsessed with VH.

I was 14, and immediately started collecting everything from posters to magazines. I even got the previous Dave-era albums within around 3 months, but none of them, in my opinion, were a match for "5150". Not only was I was obsessed with the album, but the "Live without a net" VHS was a regular player as well. It was a rare night if I didn't play it on the video player. I was in awe of everything they did. They were a different breed to any other band. I'd never seen a band perform like they did. These guys didn't just play great music, they were enjoying it. The chemistry was undeniable, and they were smiling ear-to-ear. Man, that concert was like a two-hour toothpaste commercial.

OU812 came out on my 16th birthday in '88 and, still holds a special memory in my heart. From this time on, waiting for the release day of a VH album was the most anticipating, impatient, and exciting times of my life. I knew by the day of release, I wouldn't be let down. They always delivered. From '86 to '95 were the best years of my life, and VH was the soundtrack. They were the greatest band on the earth and never disappointed.

In '96 the dreaded news hit me when Sammy left. I loved them so much I fell into depression. I knew on *Balance* something was off key, but I didn't expect it to happen so quickly. For years I was constantly waiting for the news Sammy would re-join. When Sammy toured Australia my spirits were lifted. The Melbourne gig still holds up as my favorite. Sammy was incredible that night. I was first row and I witnessed two hrs of relentless hard rock. But still, under all that excitement there was still a yearning that one day he'd re-connect with Ed and Al. Interestingly enough, VH, with Gary Cherone, toured Australia a month before and I saw them in Melbourne and Sydney.

In '03, I remember a news leak on melodic rock Sammy had met up with Al and they were talking. Even though it was early days, it was the most promising news ever, and gave me some hope these guys could do an album again and maybe tour. Well, it happened. I was pumped. As soon as news broke they would tour the U.S. from June onwards, I wasn't going to let this chance slip, I had to go. I booked to see them in St. Louis and Chicago and was on top of the world. I based myself in Ft Wayne, Ind. for 8eightweeks and travelled the U.S. while I was there. The shows lacked the punch of the previous tours, due to Ed's condition and substance abuse, but I no longer felt "cheated" they never toured Australia during the Sammy years. I finally saw them, and my prayers were answered.

In '05, Sammy's run with VH ended again, but I felt closure. I had seen Sammy twice with VH, and once with the Wabos in Melbourne. I'm still yearning for the day I can see Sammy at a birthday bash, but in these, times nothing is certain. I have been to Sammy's bar and grill in Maui though.

Sammy runs in my blood. He's not only the greatest singer ever, but he's a great and very humble man. He's passionate, spreads great inspiration, and has a connection with me, even though we've never met. I'd be truly lost without him. His way of life is always positive, and he tries to see the good in everything. He's like a religion. He's spiritual, and songs such as *Give to Live*, *Returning of the Wish*, and *Tropic of Capricorn* transport me to a different place: Maui,, Cabo, or any beach for that matter. His outlook on life runs through his family too. Velma, his sister, has tremendous vision . His 2 sons, Aaron and Andrew, and daughters Kama and Samantha.

Thank you Sammy for all the great years, but I know they are not finished yet. I've got every album. Montrose, VH, solo, etc and I'm a crazy collector. I have tattoos of you on my arms and chest to prove my fandom too. You are engraved in me.

Close Encounters of the Sammy Kind

By Tiffany Feisthamel

It all started April 23, 1992. I was 16-years-old and my mom took me to a Van Halen concert. It was a great show, but I was so impressed with Sammy Hagar. I loved his voice and his energy. I didn't know much about him until this day. During his solo he sang *Give to Live* and *Eagles Fly* and I was completely hooked. I went out the next day and bought the *I Never Said Good-bye* album. Then I bought every album I could find of Sammy's until I had every piece of music he ever recorded I could find I had lyrics from *Give to Live* tattooed on my arm with my favorite lyric of all time: "I believe in fate and destination, but so much of that lies in our own hands."

I have been able to see Sammy in concert several times and I've had four close encounters with him.

My first close encounter was in August 2000. My uncle and I went to see him in Montana. I met a lady there with a MAS TQLA license plate and started to talk to her. She said she was told to meet at the Cabo Wabo tequila bottle because she was going to get on stage. I asked her to take me with her and she did. I left everything behind with my uncle, including my ID. Turns out I needed that ID when I was signing paperwork. I asked the tour manager if my "stepmom" aka my new friend could sign for me since I didn't have my ID. You could tell he knew we were telling a little white lie, but he agreed. So yeah, I got to be on stage behind David Lauser. Sammy came and interacted with the crowd. I was wearing my Red Rocker shirt and he said "nice shirt". He signed my new friend's license plate. That's how I learned that I needed to get a Sammy-themed license plate. It was great to be on stage and close to Sammy. My uncle took some great pictures too.

My second close encounter was November 2004 when Van Halen did their reunion tour. I was lucky enough to win Golden Ring tickets. Our radio station had people send in essays as to why they deserved to win the tickets. I did a play on song titles for mine. It took them until the last day of ticket giveaways to call me and I was at work. I told them *It's About Time*, but I'm not sure they got my play on another song title. I brought my CNTDR55 license plate to the concert. When Sammy came over to our section I held it up and he came over and signed it. Later in the show, he started to play the first chords of *I Can't Drive 55 and* turned around and looked at me. I held up my license plate. He came over, held it up for the entire audience, handed it back to me, and proceeded to play the song.

My third close encounter was August 2012 at The Vinyl at the Hard Rock Hotel in Las Vegas. I met Vic, Mona, and David that night. My husband and I even hung out with Vic before Sammy came in. One of our new friends we had made bought Vic a Jagermeister shot. He said he doesn't do shots so he drank it slowly...and hated every minute of it. After a bit the crowd swarmed and I knew Sammy had entered the room. I decided to join the swarm. I had seen several people just go straight for a hug from Sammy so I decided to do the same. I couldn't believe I had actually just hugged Sammy Hagar. Later, Sammy came over to our table and posed for some pictures with me and signed my *Guitar Magazine* I had brought with him on the cover. We watched him receive the Voice of Rock award the next night.

My fourth Sammy Hagar encounter was a good one. As you can imagine, by now everyone who knows me knows that I'm a huge Sammy Hagar Fan. In October 2020 I had a friend message me because she had found out Sammy and Guy were going to be in Big Sky December 4, 2020 at Lone Mountain Ranch.

Her message to me: «Tiffany! No one is supposed to know this but I HAVE TO TELL YOU! Sammy Hagar and Guy Fieri have a sleigh ride reservation at Lone Mountain Ranch Dec. 4. At first I was like why does this have to happen during a pandemic? But then I decided to figure out if it was going to be possible to even go. My husband and I decided to take a drive to Big Sky one weekend and scope out Lone Mountain Ranch so I'd know where I needed to be. I then took a day off work to see if I'd have any luck just getting a peek of them.

When I arrived they were no where to be seen, so after wandering around for a few minutes I went back to my truck. As soon as I sat down in my truck I looked ahead and saw Guy's hair I was just in that area so I just missed them So I grabbed my SANTO license plate I had taken off the truck the night before (just in case) and walked over to where Sammy and Guy were. I was super excited and nervous. I watched them get their pictures taken with the new Santo Reposado bottle. Sammy was playing and singing *Santa's Going South for Christmas.* It was just so fun to watch from afar.

As they were finishing up the photo shoot I saw Sammy come over to the fire pit to warm up. I wasn't far from it so I said "Hi Sammy". That's when he walked over to me and said "hi". He asked me if I was alone. When I said "yes" he invited me to hang out with them, but one of the Santo people reminded him he had an interview in a minute so he said that we needed to take pictures. I showed him my license plate and he yelled to Guy that "we have a super fan over here". After Guy came over, they both were so kind to stop what they were doing and pose for pictures. I showed Sammy my tattoo I have with lyrics from *Give to Live* and we did a tattoo pose. I also couldn't resist having Sammy do the love-sign pose with me he always does with Michael Anthony. The entire Santo crew was so nice I unfortunately forgot how to speak so I didn't get to say a lot of things I wanted to, but it was the most amazing Sammy experience to date. Thank you Sammy for always taking time for your fans.

Everyone who knows me knows I am a huge Sammy Hagar fan. In October 2020, I had a friend message me because she had found out Sammy and Guy were going to be in Big Sky on Dec. 4, 2020 at Lone Mountain Ranch.

I, of course, had to take that day off work to see if I could get a peek at them. When I arrived, they were no where After wandering around for a few minutes, I went back to my truck and I looked ahead and saw Guy's hair. I was just there. How did I miss them?

I grabbed my SANTO license plate, I had taken off the truck the night before, (just in case) and walked over to Sammy and Guy. I was super excited and so nervous. I was shaking.

I watched them get their pictures taken with the new Santo Reposado bottle. Sammy was playing and singing *Santa's Going South for Christmas*. It was just so fun to watch from afar.

As they were finishing up the photo shoot, I saw Sammy go over to the fire pit to warm up.I said hello to Sammy and he walked over to me. I showed him my license plate and he yelled to Guy a super fan was there.

After Guy came over, they both were kind to stop what they were doing and pose for a bunch of pictures with me. I showed Sammy my tattoo I have with lyrics from *Give to Live so* we did a tattoo pose.

That wasn't my first Sammy experience. In 2004, when Van Halen did the reunion tour, I was lucky enough to win Golden Ring tickets. Our radio station had people send in essays as to why they deserved to win the tickets. I did a play on song titles for mine.

I brought my CNTDR55 license plate to the concert. When Sammy came over to our section, I held it up and he came over and signed it.

Later in the show, during his solo, he started to play the first chords of *I Can't Drive 55 and* turned around and looked at me. I held up my license plate, he came over, held it up for the entire audience to see, handed it back, and proceeded to play the song.

In 2012, Sammy was promoting his Beach Bar Rum at the new Vinyl at the Hard Rock Hotel and receiving the Voice of Rock award in Las Vegas. I was lucky enough to be selected to get tickets.

When he came into The Vinyl he was swarmed, so I took advantage and got a hug from Sammy. He later came over and posed for pictures and signed a *Guitar* magazine I had with him on the cover. We also hung out with Vic for a bit at the show and I met all the Wabos and Kari too. It was a whirlwind, but so fun to get to meet Sammy up close and personal for the first time.

Musings

By Toni Anderson

My parents are diehard REDHEADS. From birth Sammy's music has been blasted in our home, leaving a lasting imprint on our hearts. Dad passed away in a motorcycle accident a couple of weeks before we were supposed to go see Sammy in concert, so we said our good-byes at his funeral RED ROCKER style with some Chickenfoot. Since then, we have traveled near and far to make as many shows as possible with my mom. The way she glows and is covered with goosebumps during Sammy shows is very contagious. We have four generation ages of RED ROCKER monsters. There are no words to thank Sammy for all the memories.

By Bruce Mears

I grew up in the country with little to no exposure to rock music. At age 18, (1979), I went to my first concert. It was Boston at the Spectrum in Philly. Some guy I had never heard of named Sammy Hagar led off. I left the show a Hagar fan. I've made it to every Sammy tour except the last Chickenfoot tour. I saw Sammy on my 50th birthday at the House of Blues in New Orleans. Of course, I've been to Cabo too, as well as the first Cabo cruise. I saw two shows at The Strat in Vegas with VIP meet and greet.

By Ron Moore

In 1981, I was 18 years old and attended a concert at The Country Club in Reseda, Ca. The headliner was Gamma, Ronnie Montrose's band at the time. I had been a Montrose fan since 1976 and was an aspiring guitarist influenced by him as well. Well, right after Gamma's show, I talked my way backstage telling security I just wanted to meet and speak to Ronnie for a college journalism project. When I got backstage, I saw a large group of people gathered around a table with everyone smiling and having a good time. I walked closer to the group of people and suddenly, I was standing face to face with Sammy Hagar. I'm sure I looked surprised and dumbfounded. Before I could get any words out, Sammy patted me on my shoulder like he knew and said "Hey, how's it going?" Oh my! We proceeded to talk for a few minutes with a couple of others joining in. I've got to say he was/is the first and friendliest rock star I have ever met and will never forget that. I'm so happy for all his success on everything he's done even outside of the rock biz.

By Glenn Nicholson

In 1992, I saw you guys in a Hartford, CT concert. It was the night before my real analysis exam at Eastern CT State University. I had a little guilt that I should be studying instead of rocking it out with you guys. Sometimes in life you just say, "Fuck it"! I still managed to get a B on the exam. The show was incredible. I love you guys and definitely missing Eddie. I have a sports and rock memorabilia room in my condo. In this gallery I have many pictures all over the wall, some autographed.

By Reid Pellicer

I met Sammy recently in St. Augustine at a meet and greet. I had the *5150* record cover in my hand and he signed it for me. It was an experience I will never forget.

The Story of the Hat
By Wayne Widner

Hi, I'm Wayne, husband of Gretta. I have been music fan ever since Elvis showed up and opened the door for Sammy. Then I got lucky and married Gretta.Thank goodness she likes music. Our first date was a trip to to see Toby Keith. She kept talking about Sammy, and Van Halen. We have made several trips to Dallas, San Antonio, Mississippi, and Arkansas to see Sammy shows.

We flew to Cabo for Sammy's Birthday Bash in 2008. We made another trip to Cabo to see if we missed anything. The HAT first showed up at the 2015 NASCAR track in Ft. Worth at the Sammy show on the race track. Sammy put on The HAT and wore it while singing. After all, it's a cowboy hat and he was in Texas. This was the first time he signed The HAT. In 2021 we made it to Vegas. Back in Texas, The HAT made two more Sammy shows. Not sure how many times Sammy signed The HAT but a lot. Keep it up and hang more in Texas.

The Day My Wife's Boobs saved Sammy Hagar

By Timothy Cornish

It was a hot summer night, July 7th, 2006. It was the *Living it up* tour and happened to be Vic Johnson's birthday. Still my favorite concert to date.My buddy and I both got two tickets each for "On Stage Funatics" risers, which are typically limited to 25 people. We both took our wives to this amusement park/outdoor venue. With the living it up tour, they had a mini fair set up outside of the pavilion area having a carnival-type party prior to the show. We got there early to enjoy the Waborita's and festivities. Being one of the first couple hundred people through the gates, we received giant Sombreros as free souvenirs, (mind you, this is an important part of the story, and I do still have these sombreros to this day). They had garbage cans full of pre-made Waboritas, a dunk tank with local strippers getting dunked, side-stage for local bands, and people giving out Cabo Wabo tequila temporary tattoos.

So getting on-stage is a great experience, but an expensive one too. You arrive at a side gate 40 minutes prior to show so you can sign a waiver, get your lanyard credentials, be escorted to the risers, and wait for the curtain draw. My buddy and our wives were not able to sprint to a railing like others, so we took our place at the top center of the riser behind David Lauser. The unique thing about the risers; they had two steps. One on the railing/stage side, and a second step up behind the stage. We stood on the second step higher up to get better pictures.

If you were lucky enough to see this tour, there were two halves of the show. The first half performed by Sammy and The Waboritas consisted of 13 songs, including *Rock Candy*, which had Johnson playing one of the most memorable solos ever. After closing up the first half with *Heavy Metal,* they took a short 15-minute intermission before the second half of the bill. It was "Sammy Hagar and the other Half", which was Michael Anthony taking over for Mona, and they played nothing but Van Halen songs, only to close the show with an encore of the Beastie Boys *Fight for your Right.*

Now this is when those sombrero's came into play. These things were huge, and there were four of us, so we stacked our four sombrero's and placed them on the first step riser, and we were standing above them. The band ripped into *Best of Both Worlds,* the point in the show where Sammy walks up through the risers high-fiving everyone. When he gets through people, he marches them on stage, to circle around back to the risers. Sammy is squeezing and maneuvering while singing. The bodyguard had his hand on Sammy and stayed close. Halfway through, Sammy got to us and tripped over the pile of sombreros. The impressive thing is Sammy, instead of falling, he leapt to land on the second step of the riser where we were. My buddy and I tried to grab Sammy but ended catching the bodyguard. Sammy landed in front of my wife, but had to reach out and grab something to keep from falling. To our surprise, Sammy's hand ended up on my wife's breast. She grabbed his arm and helped him balance. Sammy looked embarrassed, stopped, covered his face, and hugged my wife saying, "I'm so sorry". Sammy was so genuine. My wife turned to us and said: "Sammy just grabbed my boob." She felt honored that it happened, and left us with a memory that will last forever.

The Adventures of Sammy

By Tommy Gerbic

My Sammy "story" is not so much a story, but an adventure. I first saw Sammy live with ZZ Top at the Richfield Coliseum in 1983. I must admit as a big ZZ Top fan that Sammy wasn't the "big draw" for me. At that time, the truth is, I was more familiar with Iron Maiden's cover of *I've Got the Fire* than Sammy's with Montrose. But as a music lover and 80's concert freak that would go see anything and everything. I was immediately impressed with Sammy's stage delivery, relatable songs, and his effort to give the fans a good performance.

After the show I quickly gobbled up his entire solo and Montrose library. I know sometimes Sammy gets knocked for his simple lyrics, less poetic and more straightforward storytelling, but I call bullshit. Those songs strike a chord in one's every-day life. Live free, have fun, enjoy, experience, travel and love.

Relatable, I had a 1978 Trans Am as a teenager so the songs, *Trans Am*, *My Baby's on Fire* were real. *Make it Last*, *Bad Motor Scooter*, *Rock Candy*, the relatability never ended.

Within a few months my two favorite artists were Van Halen and Sammy. Never a huge Roth guy but still love Rothe era VH for the music. As soon as all the stuff with Roth went down, I was screaming for Van Halen to recruit Sammy. It was as if the music Gods heard my plea. I remember working on my Trans Am with a buddy in his garage when I heard Sammy was joining VH. I told my friend Rusty (R.I.P. buddy) They are going to kick ass, and soar to new heights. When I first heard *Why Can't This Be Love* on the radio, I cranked that bitch up as loud as it could go. *Hot Summer Nights* and the entire *5150* are big favorites of mine. It was always party time with Van Hagar. In one of my best friend's wedding, we did the *5150* across the dance floor.

After hearing about Cabo Wabo, I had to find out more about the place. I mean, if Sammy, Keith Richards and all these people love it, it must be something special. I made my first trip down in 1994. Fell in love, returned in '98 for the B-Day Bash and now am up to three to four trips per year and own a three-bedroom ocean-view condo.

One of my trips, a friend and I were out collecting empty tequila bottles. We got in a friendly fight at some little place and busted up the furniture. In walks Joe Montana, Sly Stallone, and Bruce Willis. They wanted nothing to do with us "loopy gringos" as the staff was calling us.

I have met Sammy numerous times at the Cantina and meet and greets. Sammy has always seemed authentic and friendly. I got a concert review on redrocker.com. I've been lucky enough to attend many b-day bashes and many shows in Ohio Spending these moments, the music, the people, the food, the drinks, and the fun at his shows and in Cabo with my beautiful wife Kristi and great friends is what life is all about.

Just a Texas Girl Who Loves Sammy

By Jill Schultz

It all started back in 1982 when a BMX buddy let me listen to the *Standing Hampton* cassette. I wore that thing out. I was only twelve or so. I had never been to a live concert before. When Sammy came around to tour, I wanted to go. My big brother said, nope. Didn't want his little sister hanging around. After a couple years I got to go to a concert finally with my friend who played me the cassette. I was hooked. A bunch of us piled into his parent's van and went to the show. Krokus opened up and then Sammy came on. From there on, I've spent all the money I could on seeing Sammy from coast-to-coast and of course, Mexico. I want to wish a Super Happy 75th Birthday to Sammy. I've enjoyed so much of my life seeing him grow up.

Musings

By Blaine B.

About three years ago, my father was visiting me in Michigan. He showed me a photo on his phone and asked if I knew who it was. I said, "That's Sammy FREAKING Hagar." But what threw me off was that the photo was taken in my dad's kitchen. They were having a celebratory cocktail together. Then he proceeded to tell me that Sammy was the new owner of my dad's house that had been up for sale. My dad and Sammy are approximately the same age. As the story goes, Kari had seen the house a couple times and loved it. But the only problem was that Sammy had too many houses and needed to sell one, so he sold his house in Hawaii and purchased my dad's house. Now every time I watch some of Sammy's videos on his Red Rocker FB page doing some of his Mixology videos, or something like that, I am like, "hey that looks familiar".

Musings

By Bob Tewksbury

It all started one night in Binghamton, NY at the Broome County Veterans Memorial Arena. Sammy was the opening act for Boston. It was my first concert experience, so he was the first performer I had ever seen in a large concert venue. I really dug Boston at the time and never even heard of Sammy. I liked seeing Boston but couldn't get the performance of Sammy and Gary Pihl out of my head, along with Gary Pihl and the Bad Motor Scooter guitar battle Bill Church and Chuck Ruff. I loved *Rock N Roll Weekend*, *Turn Up the Music*, and *RED*. The next day, I bought *All Night Long* and forgot all about BOSTON. I dove head-first into Sammy and Montrose. I was the guy who called radio stations every day to request songs. I felt it was my duty as a fan. Lost count of all the shows. Sammy memories are the best.

A Very Lucky Man

By Deb Durant

Rock 'n' Roll with the man and his guys. We just got back from Vegas and saw him open up his residency at the Strat the first night. We stood the entire show. It was fabulous. We can't wait to see him again. We went to Cabo Wabo for dinner Halloween night. First time visit and it was delish. The margaritas were out of this world. While we were at the concert, his wife was right in front of us in the audience. She's very beautiful. He's one lucky man. We tried to buy VIP tickets, but they were sold out.

Looking for a Shot

By Kerri Bernard

Every time I am in Cabo, we visit Cabo Wabo in hopes to not only hear Sammy perform, but to have a shot of tequila with him. We went in the night before Thanksgiving 2020, knowing Sammy was in town and praying he just might wander in. No luck, but we found out he appeared there on Thanksgiving and did shots with everyone. Covid rules were in place at that time so the big bar was closed and it was a limited intimate crowd in the smaller area. This was so cool for everyone that was able to be there that night. Huge Envy. I feel confident it will happen one day.

Photo Courtesy of Timothy Cornish

Freeze the Pizza

By Vince Mattias

In 1993, Van Halen played in Michigan for the **Right Here Right Now** tour. A friend of mine found out what plane the band was coming in on, so we went to the Detroit airport and waited at the gate. Eddie, Alex and Mike came off the plane. Sammy's plane landed 15 minutes later. The band signed my copy of *Guitar World* that featured Eddie as the player of the decade.

We walked with Alex Van Halen through the airport and outside as they were awaiting their limo to pick them up. I got a photo with Mike, and then a few minutes later got a photo together with Sammy and Alex. We ran to our car and followed them to the hotel. We couldn't go in though, so my buddy and I sat outside figuring out what to do next.

We walked around the hotel and saw Alex Van Halen walking with someone we didn't know. We caught up to them and it turned out to be their tour manager, Scotty Ross, walking with Alex. Al remembered us from the airport. Alex said my buddy and I would get backstage passes to the next night's show. We were absolutely floored. Then things got crazier.

Scotty turned to Al and asked how many? Al said, four", then turned to us and said, "Want to eat with us?" HOLY CRAP YES! We went to a pizza restaurant. Al and Scotty each ordered a pizza. We talked about a the tour and songs. I could only take one bite of the pizza because I was so nervous. After dinner, they boxed up the pizza. Al says: "You didn't eat, so take this home". I actually put it in my freezer and saved it for six months.

We walked back to the hotel and my buddy told them he made a version of Eddie's Frankenstein guitar and wondered if Eddie would sign it. Alex told him to get the guitar. We were right outside the hotel, and I noticed Sammy and Kari were walking out from dinner and said something like "Hey, there's Sammy."

He was now standing with his back to us, waiting for the elevator to come down and open up. Al says, "Flip off Sammy". I told him I couldn't do that. He said: "If you want to come backstage tomorrow, you have to flip him off now".

The elevator opened and Sammy and Kari walked in and turned around. There's me, Scotty and Alex are all flipping the bird. Sammy looked confused. The elevator closed and my buddy showed up with his car with the guitar in the trunk. Al and Scotty looked at the guitar and then I heard yelling above.

Sammy came out on the balcony and yelled, "You buying drugs from these guys? What's with you guys flipping me off man?" He laughed and Al said something while Scotty and I looked at the guitar. Well, the guys went inside and my buddy and I drove 45 minutes home, screaming in the car about what we just experienced.

The next day we went to Pine Knob and got to go backstage. I gave Alex a cassette copy of Van Halen playing at a high school in 1976. Sammy remembered me from the night before and said, "Wait, you were at the hotel, wtf with the fingers?" I told him, "I didn't want to do that, Al put me up to it." He looked at Alex and laughed. Met Eddie and Mike too. Saw the band 13th row dead center that day. Two days I will never forget.

Fast forward to the 1995 *Balance* tour. The band played in Michigan again and, on my own, I got four tickets in the front row in front of Eddie. I stayed in line for two days and won the lottery to be first in line. I always dreamed of catching the guitar pic Eddie would throw during his guitar solo. I was ready. He threw the pic and bounced off my hair and went behind me — gone.

The band came out for an encore and before they started, Eddie grabbed a pic to give to me. Some guy behind me pushed me and got the pic. Eddie grabbed another pic, but the same frenzy happened and someone else got it. So Eddie went and grabbed a handful of picks from his mic stand. He knelt down at the end of the stage and my buddies tried to push me up, but security was not blocking. Sammy came over and said to security, "Hey guys, give this kid a break, help him over a bit." They did and Eddie dropped four pics into my hand.

Now this was the era when the jumbo screen was being used. When the show ended, we were going to leave and, the tour manager, came up and said, "Hello." I couldn't believe he remembered me. But he saw me from the stage and on the jumbo screen .

The next day was Easter Sunday and Scotty said, "Come back tomorrow. I'll get you tickets and passes." The next day I brought my sister to the show and we went backstage. We were the last pair of people going back for a meet and greet. We walked in and my sister heard someone say my name. I thought I did too but was so overwhelmed again, I just kept focusing on what was around me. I thanked Eddie for the guitar pics from last night and Sammy said: "You were having some troubles with that." My sister and I were the only ones there, so we got a few extra moments. The photo I got from that night is my favorite because everyone had a really good smile on their faces. My sister was in shock my name was used. I was too.

I got to meet Sammy one more time in 1995. A funny thing happened. My friend was wearing a pair of sunglasses that flipped up. I was between Eddie and Alex, when all I heard was "Oh Fuck, sorry," as a pair of sunglasses went flying. Turns out Sammy tried to lower my friend's glasses and they flipped off. Sammy scurried to get them, and put them right back on my friends face. I have seen Sammy in concert on just about every tour. Rock on Sammy and thank you for the music and all the memories.

The Best Proposal in Rock and Roll History

By Chris Massie

It's been 42 years and more than 61 shows, I've seen Sammy in all his different bands. Sammy's solo work after Montrose, Van Halen, The Waboritas, Chickenfoot, The Circle and, just this past weekend, the Tres Gusanos in Vegas.

My First show in1979, in Johnson City Tenn. Sammy. I was hooked and have officially been a REDHEAD ever since.

One story happened in Knoxville, Tenn., during the *5150* tour. I was front row and MTV kept talking about how the die-hard David Lee Roth fans were still booing and that pissed me off. I took a poster of DLR and spray painted the "I can't drive 55" circle, a slash over DLR's face, with more expletives in big red letters. I handed the poster to Sammy and he opened it up, then had one of the roadies tape it to Eddie's amp. He gave me a pic and a high five. I was on cloud nine.

My BIG Sammy story happened in 2008, during the Kenny Chesney's *Poets and Pirates* tour in Atlanta. My girlfriend and I went. I had it planned to throw Sammy a banner on stage. It was prearranged that he would hold it up. It was a proposal to ask my girlfriend, Deanna, to marry me. Sammy held it up, then proceeded to tie the banner around his waist, and wear it like a toga for the next few songs. He then handed the banner back to one of the stage guys and they brought the banner back to me. Of course, she said yes, and we just celebrated our 13th anniversary in Vegas at Sammy show number 61.

He took my sign from me that said: "THIS IS MY 61st SAMMY SHOW. CAN WE DO A SHOT OF SANTO?" and held it up for all to see. He shook my hand, brought me a BIG shot of Santo and shook my hand again. A night I will not forget. Sammy loves his fans and that's why his fans love him. Thank you, Sammy for helping me propose to my best friend and giving us an awesome engagement story. I refer to it to as the best proposal in ROCK N ROLL HISTORY. You have been the soundtrack of my life and your music

Did She Drink the Rum?

By Azalea Millet

First time Roly and I saw Sammy live was at the I Heart Radio album release party for The Circle, in Los Angeles, May 2019. We won tickets to get in and got a meet 'n' greet. I immediately felt a great vibe among fans and met some amazing Redheads while waiting in line.

That night I got a hug from Sammy and he also gave me his cup of Beach Bar Rum from the stage, which of course I still have. That's when I became a Redhead. I booked a trip to Cabo and, even though we didn't get tickets for the bday bash, we still had a blast hanging outside the Cabo Wabo.

We went to a couple more events Sammy had in LA. The Grammy Museum, where Roly got to ask Sammy a question, went to to the Eddie Money tribute, where I got my first Sammy autograph. Sammy is always so generous with his fans. It's one of the many reasons he rocks.

In 2021, I won the bday bash lottery for Catalina Island and we went for all three nights. Got some stuff autographed by Sammy and the band and, again, met some really cool people. We got to do it again in Vegas at The Strat, a month later. I have had one of the best times of my life at Sammy shows with all the great friends that I have made along the way. Moral of the story... SAMMY ROCKS & REDHEADS RULE. HAPPY BIRTHDAY SAMMY.

Musings

By Charlotte Bone

I'm a very young 60. Been listening to Sammy my entire life, from Montrose to Sammy solo, to Sammy with Van Halen, to Sammy with The Circle. Sammy is the most fun, most energetic, most party concert, which is why I keep on going and going and going. More than 20 times now if not more. I love he is a great family guy, great businessman, great friend, and lives life large. He is the rock icon I've always wanted to meet and have a drink and personally thank for the joy he has given me.

Cabo Wabo in Our Backyard

By Brandon and Susan Clark

The year was 1991, It was the *For Unlawful Carnal Knowledge Tour.* it was our first concert date at Pacific Amphitheatre in Costa Mesa, Calif.. Thirty years later, we are married with four beautiful children and Sammy is our guy. We saw him live at his 70th Birthday Bash in Cabo. We made our own Clark Cabo Wabo Bar in our backyard, where we serve Santo and Sammy serves drinks with us. We went to Catalina for the 74th birthday and just got back from Vegas VIP at the Strat. Hubby and I are still smiling from the show. Sammy brought us amazing years of music, energy, and his smile.

Musings

By Christopher Fredrickson

I became a fan of Sammy on my 15th Birthday when in 1995, I got to see him play with Van Halen. That show inspired me to learn the guitar. One of the first songs I learned was the acoustic version of *Eagles Fly.* I have followed Sammy's career ever since. The funny thing is when we went to the show, my dad is a James Taylor-kinda guy, always wearing a suit and tie. Afterwards he said: "Can you make me a tape of some of the Van Halen and Sammy Hagar stuff?" Then 25 years later we saw Sammy again together in St. Augustine.

He became a fan. I picked back up the guitar again a month after that show I have a decent following on my You Tube channel and I'm now known as"the rock and roll rabbi.

The Two-Sided Shirt

By Christopher Saylor

It was June 22, 1988. I was 15-years-old, and my sister took me to one of my first concerts The Monsters Of Rock in Philadelphia. It was Kingdom Come, Scorpions, Dokken, Metallica and Van Halen. I was excited to see Dokken and Metallica. I did not really listen to Van Halen, as much as the others as I was into heavier music.

Van Halen closed the show and the second Eddie jumped on stage, I was mesmerized and became a fan for life. Eddie brought me to Sammy and I followed him throughout the band break-up and continued with his solo and the Wabos part of his career.

I went to every near-by show and eventually attended the birthday bash in Cabo. I was hooked on Sammy's music, the vibe, and lifestyle he portrayed. I would wait after the shows for years to try to get a handshake, a wave, hello, picture, or a signature to no avail. I went to Cabo in 2008 for a CD release party at the Cantina. The band was supposed to be there. I thought: "Oh my God this is it. I'm finally gonna meet him."

The Wabos were there; Mona, Vic, and Dave, but no Sammy. I met them, talked, and got them to sign my shirt. They performed and when Sammy arrived everyone was lined up by the wall, where he walks from the car to the Cantina. I ran over; when he walked by, I got a hand-slap. I smiled the rest of the night. The split-second it took to slap a hand was all I needed. I still needed a picture or signature to complete my shirt.

I continued to stay after shows, but it wasn't until I went to a show in Atlantic City, N.J. There was a Sammy's Beach Bar on the beach. A manager indicated he would be coming by to make a donation to a food bank. After he presented the check I was able to get a picture with Sammy. I was still on the hunt for the last shirt signature. But it wasn't until two years later in Pennsylvania at a show and he was signing things. My wife demanded me to give her the shirt and she was able to run to the stage and get it signed. He signed it the opposite side of the Wabos. I made a double-sided display for the shirt to see all the signatures. I want to thank Sammy for all that he has done and all the music that means so much to me.

A Winning Combination

By Connie Mitchell

In 1994 my friend won tickets to a Dallas concert by winning a cake contest Vince Neal judged. When the radio host at the contest found out Vince did not come to congratulate her, he said he would make sure she met the opening band Motley Crüe.

The radio host got us into the meet and greet before the concert. Motley Crüe came in and they made us kneel on the floor in front of them for a picture.

They left and in came Van Halen. Sammy arrived with Eddie, Mike, and Alex and right away was friendly. It was a surreal moment.

We were both pregnant at the time, my friend and I. Sammy came up to us and offered us a beer. I looked at my friend and exclaimed one beer won't hurt us, and we cannot turn down a beer from Sammy. When it was picture time, they did not make us kneel on the floor, instead, we were arm-in-arm. This is when I got the Sammy bug. He was so nice and kind and made two pregnant gals happy. Truly a night to remember.

In 2012. I bought VIP tickets to celebrate my 50th birthday. When Sammy and the gang came in for a meet and greet, they were so down-to-earth and genuine nice guys all around. Sammy gave me a hug and I asked him if he had received a Chickenfoot stained-glass piece I sent to him. He said, "That was 'you'? As a matter of fact, yes, and it hangs in my studio." That made my night to know a piece of my glass artwork was hanging in his studio. I thought the night could not get any better, but I was proposed to that evening. A month later, June 29, 2012, we got married. I have seen Sammy many times and even attended his wife's 50th birthday bash in Cabo. Sammy Hagar is truly a one-of-a-kind person. It shows in how he treats his fans and all the good things he does. We all love him.

Musings

By Madalene Rivera

I met Sammy at the Hard Rock Café, in San Francisco in the early '80s. He was doing a promo for radio station KRQR. My best friend and I were there early in the morning. It was pouring down rain. We were greeted by one of the set-up guys. We talked and he told us to say we were his cousins and he'd get us a meet with Sammy. It was one of the most memorable moments of my life. I have loved Sammy's music since I first listened to a Montrose album when I was 17. Been in love ever since. When I heard the song *RED*, I was elated as that has always been my favorite color. Happy 75th birthday. May your music live on forever.

By Marci Jeffrey

My very first concert was a Montrose show at Winterland in San Francisco 1974. I was only 12 and went with an older guy who had a car. I was mesmerized by the whole experience and completely in awe of Sammy. I'm originally from the Bay area and feel like I've grown up with Sammy. Best moment was July 2018 when he showed up at Cabo Wabo. I just happened to be there too. Got my bucket list picture with him.

By Nick Cianelli

Me and my wife, Susan, were at the Lake Tahoe show 2015. Sammy signed our unopened bottle of Cabo Uno, as well as the box We have met Sammy several times throughout the 2000s. I have been an up-front fanatic at more than 30 shows and have been in several videos including *Mas Tequila*, (where Sammy signed my unopened Cabo Uno bottle), and *Divine Termination, where* Chad Smith gave us his bass drum skin. We have traveled coast-to-coast to get rocked by Sammy and will continue to do so.

The Mustang Tattoo

By Derek Talbert

I became a Redhead as a young teen. My friend and I went to see Sammy at the Seattle Center Coliseum. This was my third big concert, but when I saw Sammy, running all over the stage, bringing out the Trans AM, and sitting, playing crazy shit on that funky little box guitar. Coolest guitar solo ever. I knew right there I would always love this man's music. Came to see him later in life, be it Van Hagar, or the Wabos, or with The Circle. He is the best. He treats his fans with the utmost respect.

My wife bought us front-row tickets for my 50th birthday. Sam looked down at me and gave me a high-five. Then he saw I was wearing a red-and-black Mustang hat. I tossed it up to him, and he put it on and talked about owning Mustangs. He wore my hat for two more songs. He signed my hat and made sure I got it back. Then my wife took it, put on her head, and said: "OMG I have Sammy DNA on me." It was the top of our rock 'n' roll experience life!! The hat and Sammy autograph turned into a tat.

Thought that experience could never be topped, we then we did a Vegas meet and greet with Sammy. I thought he would see my hat, and then I would show him my Mustang, 'Sammy I can't drive' tat,' and he would be like 'dude, love you so much,' but the best thing happened. He saw my wife was getting emotional, She was crying; he grabbed her hands, settled her down, gave her a kiss on the forehead, and made sure the pics were all about her. Just made him a bigger hero in my eyes. Red Head forever.

Theres a Reason for Everything

By Donna Bristow

I love when you say that! We all do! I also love when you say, “At Your Service”, and “I love this sh*t!” It shows how much you care for new and older fans alike.

I’m one of the older fans. Not too old, I started young thanks to my older brother. My first time seeing you live was in 1976, Knoxville, TN. My brother introduced me to Montrose. Rick played drums and bass guitar and he was my first hero. . I got to tell him I finally met you in November at your residency. He is in heaven now after losing his battle with cancer in December.

I went to your residency alone from SC cause my best friend, who is also a fan, was on the Kiss cruise. There is a reason for everything though, and I met some of the sweetest Redheads. One couple, Azalea and Rolondo, hugged me, cried with me, and prayed for my brother. It was so sweet. God knew I needed some friends and something to make me happy. So grateful I went to Vegas.

I followed you in the 80’s and my anthem was I Can’t Drive 55! That was my I Can’t Drive 55 mask you wore at the Strat! I was on the road a lot in sales and got lots of tickets! I remember when that stupid law came out and how much everyone hated it! Especially in SC!

Shortly after that, David Lee Roth left Van Halen. I thought that was the end of Van Halen. Even when it was announced you were the new lead singer, sadly I was skeptical. Just didn’t think you were a good fit. Boy was I stupid!!!! When 5150 came out, I was blown away! Best Van Halen album to date!!!!!! There was just magic with you in the band! Didn’t hurt you were gorgeous either!

The Van Hagar era was by far the best and so many happy memories with each song. All of these years, I had truly hoped y’all would reunite again. For now, I’m just grateful for the joy you’ve brought me since 1976 and continue to do so.

I never got to attend your birthday bash in Cabo due to work in the Fall, and you rarely play the Carolinas (not sure why, we’re begging) so I’m grateful I got to attend the residency in Nov. When I told you I waited 40 years to meet you, you had a big grin and blew me a kiss. That was worth the wait! Thank you for taking a photo with me and for being so kind! And thank you for the things you have signed from the stage.

Thank you, God, for giving us Sammy for 75 years and more! Happy birthday, Sammy! Thank you for the music and thank you for being you!

Much love from South Carolina

Give Me Red

By Cindy Bear

It was the summer of 1999. I stayed up all night with my sister-in-law trying to figure out the perfect Sammy Hagar license plate for my 1967 Mustang. At 7 a.m. I screamed: "I got it!!!" GVMERED, (*Give me red*), my favorite song.

I received that plate in 2000 and took the set to a Van Halen show in Sacramento. My best friends went with me. We had seats way at the top at the Arco Arena. When we got there, I looked at all of them and said: "I'm going to the front of the stage to get Sammy to sign this plate and I'm going to give him one." My friend, said, "Let's go." My two guy friends said. "Yeah, right."

After a wild time winding through the crowd, I made it to the front of the stage and up on the railing. Sammy came right over and I gave him one plate. He put on Alex Van Halen's drum set and then the magic happened. He broke out singing *Give Me Red* and when he finished, sat at the edge of the stage, autographed my plate, and yelled, "ARCO ARENA YOU GOT RED?"

The crowd went crazy. He handed my plate back and said, "I already know you got red, girl." I was hooked from that moment on. I never sat again. I stood in line for hours to be an UPFRONT fanatic. I lied to DMV when I got home and told him they fell off on the freeway. They gave me a new set. I still have them on my car today, and bring the one Sammy signed so many years ago to every show I go.

Thanks to Sammy, for all the great times. He even played my ukulele at the Sweetwater in Mill Valley, Calif. to close his show So many memories, and kind and thoughtful things he has done for me and his fans.

Peace Sammy and Happy Birthday

Sammy Hagar Way

By Matt Slowik

Sammy, it's been a 60-year-journey, and an amazing ride. Beginning with gigs at the Fontana Community Church and Women's Club Building, to "The Bar, to the Swing Auditorium and every venue since. It has been an unmatched lifetime of grand adventures. "Are we havin' any fun yet"? Yes, we are. We all had humble beginnings growing up in Fontana, but through the decades, I was blessed to be a friend and neighbor of the Hagar's, Solis', and Harrell's.

Sammy blessed us with his music, songwriting, entertainment, fan-appreciation, and on-stage invitations. I collaborated and worked with his crew on special events including grand marshal at the 100-Year Anniversary Fontana Days Parade. As one of my last actions as a Fontana City councilman, I was proud to initiate (and gain council consensus) to have the street Sammy Hagar Way street named in his honor.

Most of all thanks to Sam for his philanthropic spirit in supporting and giving so much to children's charities and food banks. He supported first-responders, with particular interest to firefighters. He was a catalyst to the creation of the first residential fire sprinkler ordinance" in Fontana.

If we are "Red-Until-We-Are-Dead," then, we will continue to "Appreciate your Musical-Thunder until we are Six-Feet-Under"! (A Fontanaman Quote).

Happy Birthday Sam. May God continue to bless and shine his everlasting grace upon you, Kari, Kama, Samantha, Aaron, Andrew, and the entire extended family.

Sing Red for Carter

By Debbie Knutson

It was June 4,2011 and Sammy came to Tucson, Ariz.. I geared up with a special sign, a favorite song, I wanted to hear for a reason. My sign read "Sing Red for Carter". You see, Sammy's long-time manager and friend, John Carter, whom he wrote *Red* with, had passed away a few weeks earlier. The show began and what was the first song? You guessed it, *Red*. It was awesome. Sammy acknowledged my sign as he always does with everyone. Later during the show, he came over, bent down, (as I was in the front row again), and put his hands on my shoulders. He told me,:"Thank you for that sign. It really meant a lot to me". I was so thrilled. Who else does this? Only Sammy recognizes and

Photo Courtesy Mike Healey

appreciates all his fans. He signs items while singing and makes sure the person gets it back. He is the kindest, sweetest, most giving, and talented musician on earth. Later in the show we shared a margarita. What a great night.

Musings

By Shana Vetter

As a child of the '80s, growing up in the cornfields of the Midwest meant you grew up on the airwaves of KSHE 95. And that, my friends, meant a heavy dose of Sammy. From my love of Trans Ams, to my love of a good margarita, Sammy's influence is evident. More memories with KSHE 95 listeners are coming.

Photo Courtesy Blaine B.

Seat Mates

By Mike Healey

Sammy had a show coming up early 2001 at the Turning Stone Resort and Casino in Verona N.Y., a venue that holds about 800 people.

I had seen Sammy with Van Halen numerous times, but had never seen him solo. I think this was the birthday bash tour with the Wabos with Vic on guitar, Mona on bass, and David on drums. I was hesitant to go because I was worried he would not play many VH songs, and I was not too familiar with the solo catalog outside of 55 and *There's Only One Way to Rock.* The show was sold out and I had two extra tickets to sell so I didn't think it would be a problem. We get there and a couple had driven more than two hours and I gave them my tickets at face value, because that's what Redheads do. They were so happy we sat with them at the show.

Sammy began the show with *10/13.* Then played songs like *Shaka Doobie, Red, Heavy Metal, Give to Live* and *Marching to Mars.* My mind was blown. I, from that point on, did not care if he played any VH songs. From that point on I was hooked and became a true Redhead. To hear songs for the first time and be blown away was awesome.

Fast forward eight to 10 years later. Sammy was playing a show in Buffalo N.Y. When my wife and I got to our seats, the lady next to us said, "Oh my God! How are you guys?" I was a confused because she did not look familiar. She then told us about the show several years earlier in Syracuse and that they were the couple we sold our extra tickets to. Amazing that after all that time we were at another Sammy show sitting next to each other.

As I mentioned earlier, Redheads take care of other Redheads because that's what we do. Over the years since then I have never met a better group of people in my life. Every show is an opportunity to meet some of the best people ever.

I am proud to call myself a Redhead and look forward to meeting more of you in the future. Cabo is still on my bucket list. I was able to cross off meeting Sammy and the rest of the guys in October 2021 in Las Vegas.

It Was 'Not' By Accident

By Melissa Diomedes

When it comes to music in my life, I have been passionate about two things: Sammy Hagar and KSHE 95. Dedication that sometimes goes beyond all common sense.

In 2017 I had my first trip to Cabo planned for the Birthday Bash. I was traveling as part of the KSHE group from St. Louis and Sammy was playing in St. Louis Sept. 30, the last show before heading to Cabo. I was "rocking from the Arch to Arch" with Sammy and NOTHING was gonna stop me. I had T-shirts made, and even got my CABO WABO tattoo.

But everything was put in jeopardy the morning of Sept. 29, when I was involved in a multi-vehicle accident totaling my van and two cars. I was thrown out of my seat into the back of the van, knocked out, and covered in glass. When the police asked if I wanted to go to the hospital, all I wanted to know was what time it was. Not because I was confused, but because KSHE was having a drawing for front-row seats to the St. Louis Sammy show at 10 a.m. I needed to know if I had time to make it there before the drawing. Against my boyfriend's advice, I ignored the shoulder pain, skipped the ER and we made it to KSHE before 10 a.m. I didn't win tickets that day, but I made it to the show the next night (continuing to ignore pain). Nothing was going make me miss this Sammy show.

After a fantastic concert I did go to the ER. I did have some spleen damage and spent the next 3 days in the hospital. I was released in time to make the trip to Cabo. Sammy autographed my tattoo. I am very thankful it all worked out because this trip wasn't just a great vacation, but the starting point to some of my greatest friendships.

St. Louis Redhead

By Sheila Bates

I am an original St. Louis Redhead but have lived in Kansas City for more than 20 years now. I grew up with pretty strict Christian parents, so I didn't start "rebelling" and listening to rock until I was about 13, (1982), when we got cable TV & I got my MTV. A friend introduced me to *Standing Hampton* about the time *Three Lock Box* came out. I then started listening to KSHE-95 and got acquainted with Montrose and old-school Red Rocker. When the VOA tour came around, my parents said I wasn't old enough to go to the concert. I was so jealous of all my friends and their concert T's. I saw Sammy and Eddie rocking at Farm-Aid and I was sold. When *5150* came out at midnight, I lied to my parents, told them I was working, but was standing in line for my album. I went home, put it on cassette, so I could listen to it in my car. (No cassette deck, had to carry a boom box.) My second concert was *5150*, floor tickets in St. Louis. I didn't get to go to *OU812,* since I was a young mom with no money, but never missed a Van Halen tour since, (Including 2004 in multiple cities). I've seen Sammy (Wabos/Chickenfoot/Circle) as much as I could, since the VH break up — even been on stage a couple times. I haven't made it to a Birthday Bash yet, but Vegas was awesome. I had so many things I wanted to say to Sammy at the meet and greet; like I have an original Cabo Wabo Tequila bottle I won't open unless he shares it with me. I couldn't get anything out except, "I love you!" and gave him a huge hug, shaking the entire time. Luckily, my spouse picked me up and thanked him for all the memories and music. He even told him his Amazon Music Playlist should be called the "Samazon" account. Sammy loved that. I'm counting the days until I'm a front-row fanatic again. Happy 75th Sammy, here's to many more.

Photo Courtesy of Connie Mitchell

Stained glass art piece she made for Sammy that hangs in his studio.

What Dreams are Made of

By Gayle Bowen

Hey Sammy, my late husband Randy and myself have been fans of yours since Montrose. We were fortunate enough to see you in concert at Riverbend in Cincinnati, Huber Heights in Columbus, and The Taft Auditorium in Cincinnati, which was our last concert together. We drank Cabo and had too good of a time. You know what I mean. Sammy, you sounded so great! The acoustics were awesome! Randy was in a Rock band called Freefall in the early eighties. He was the lead singer. He loved it and was a good singer. We always wanted to go to Cabo, but it just didn't work out. Randy passed on January 13, 2008 Your music was played; Bad Motor Scooter and the acoustic version of Where Eagles Fly. I listened to Where Eagles Fly over and over while I was sitting alone. It was very comforting.

I also went to the concert where it was supposed to be a battle between you and David Lee Roth. There were four friends, myself, and my late husband Randy. There was no battle. You won hands down. David Lee Roth was so full of himself. We have enjoyed listening to your music and going to what concerts we could. I'll be going to your concert on the 24th of August at Riverbend. I'm a Kentucky girl but would cross the river anytime to see your concert!

Sammy I am glad you are enjoying your life. Thank you for all the great music!

Keep on Rocking Red Rocker!

Best wishes and happy birthday Sammy on October 13th! Keep on rocking!

Gayle Bowen

Musings

By Colin McDougal

After reading Sammy's book, I became an even bigger fan of the man. His carefree, fun loving, dedicated lifestyle of music, fast cars, love, and booze, (good booze), is what living is all about. The Red Rocker has given us that stress-free attitude in a time of world uncertainty and mixes it up with some Beach Rum and shooter of Cabo Wabo. For a Canadian East coast lad, I'm thankful for the Internet so we can tune in and be inspired by him. One day, I hope to catch up with 'The Red Rocker,' which is my signature drink.

Rocking Comes from the Womb

By Gretta Widner

It was 1979 when I met my future husband. He loved Van Halen, Hagar, Boston, and the good stuff. He was the first person who introduced me to Sammy and *Bad Motor Scooter* and I was hooked. Hagar music makes me feel like nothing else has. It sends chills down my whole body. There is no other drug or booze that makes me feel this good. It's kinda strange that I get so excited as if it were the first time. Adrenaline rushing, can't eat, can't be still.

In the summer of 1980, we went to the Texas Jamm. It was my first Sammy show. Only problem: I was pregnant. I decided to get to the front, only to be escorted to the EMT tent. Loss of oxygen. As the EMT's carried me out of the crowd, I saw my husband fade into it. After a few breaths of oxygen, I was ready to rock some more. That baby is now more than 40 and a Redhead fan. Friends say: "her rocking comes from the womb."

More shows followed, some in the nosebleed section I vowed to never do again. My daughter at 16 and I stood in line for a free show, ended up with four tickets and gave to another couple in line. It's all about love and sharing when it comes to being a true REDHEAD.

My current husband (Wayne-Elvis) has been pretty awesome. We went to Cabo, stood in line early morning, got tickets in 2004. I get Cabo. So peaceful and beautiful. I have a Cabo Wabo Yamaha guitar. Don't know a thing about playing, but if ever do I want to rock. Hope to get it signed someday. Traveling with it makes me nervous.

So many shows but Texas Motor Speedway on Nov. 8, 2015, the day before my birthday, was a highlight when I threw my hat at you to be signed. Then I got to go the next week with my daughters. Two shows in one week. I have continued going to at least two shows a year. I am addicted.

Somewhere, in there I found time to have another daughter. Now with two granddaughters, the whole family went to a show in Oklahoma. One granddaughter drew a picture "way down south where big blue agave grow." Sammy showed it to the crowd and signed it. People say I'm brain-washing them with Sammy music. The children are 45, 40, 35, 23,12, all beautiful and yes, beautifully brain-washed into Hagar music.

Vegas presented a chance to meet Mrs. Hagar and do a meet and greet. Then there were more shows in Texas. Seven shows in three months. I have been to at least 50 shows and they keep on coming.

Hope you Have the Greatest Blessed Birthday Ever.Hope you never get old. We love you just like you are. Can't wait for future journeys in my RED WORLD!!!

Photo Courtesy Nick Cianelli

The Red Rocker Rider

By Christopher Healthcoat

The first time I ever heard Sammy was the electrifying previews to a first-ever RATED-R cartoon *HEAVY METAL*. Immediately I was a fan. Then came Van Halen, and he became the soundtrack of my life. I re-cemented my vows with him as he arm-wrestled my favorite actor and did the hit song for the movie *Over The Top*. For my 50th b-day as another first, the Sammy Hagar bicycle entered my life. I made a website dedicated to this bicycle. Check red rockers.com for some action.

Photo cover of the website
Courtesy of Christopher Healthcoat

Musings

By David Gehris

Me, my wife and brother-in-law had tickets to a show. When I walked in we were invited to be in a contest. All my friends and coworkers call me Sammy. I was up with nine other people on the stage and won first prize; front row, dead center for me and my wife. It was the best night I ever had at a concert. Sammy and the Wabos looked down at me and gave me thumbs up. My wife said, “Did you see that?” I said, “See what?” A girl lifted her top but I missed it. As we were leaving, all kinds of people were asking me if they could take a picture with me and of course I said sure like I always do when I play out or go to a concert. The one thing I always regretted was not being able to get a picture of me and Sammy. We tried again in Vegas but everywhere I go people think Im Sammy and take pictures of me.

By Dan Grace

My wife took me to Sammy's show in Oklahoma for his 70th birthday bash. I'm honored to have been born on the 13th of Rocktober, just like Sammy. We paid extra to get meet and greet and on stage for the show. It was awesome. While on stage, I got pictures of me and Sammy, side-by-side. He autographed my wife's breast and handed us a bottle of his tequila. What a great night.

First, and foremost, Happy 75th Birthday Sammy!!

By Lola Ann Whitaker

Your music, energy, and positive outlook on life has helped me so much over the years. It's hard to express exactly how much you influence everyone's lives, especially mine, but I will try through this message. One of my dreams has been to meet and tell you what your music has done for me. Well, part of that dream came true on November 13, 2021, at the Strat in Las Vegas when I met you, and you commented on my KSHE shirt and curly hair. I literally cried and could hardly believe it when I had purchased those tickets for the VIP Meet & Greet. I previously met you at the book signing for Red in St. Louis and waited hours in line for just a moment with you, but at that time I couldn't even talk (you did give me a high five though). I have been to numerous concerts in St. Louis, Cabo, Chicago, and Tulsa, and I have never been disappointed with any of them. This opportunity has granted me the chance to share my story and your music's impact on me through the years.

In June 2012, my life changed unexpectedly with diagnosis of Stage 1 Breast Cancer, and my trip to the 65th Birthday Bash had already been booked. Not only was I worried about my health and the next steps, but the possibility of not being able to make the trip in October. I kept my diagnosis private except for immediate family since it was difficult for me to accept in the beginning. Through every test at this time, my choice of music was always yours to keep me calm & distracted from what was happening. Luckily after all the tests and surgery, my treatment only consisted of radiation, and my doctors arranged my treatment to start earlier than expected. This allowed my treatment to be completed a couple days before leaving for Cabo to celebrate your birthday and see my favorite musician at a couple shows. Not only did I not allow cancer to stop me from attending that birthday bash, but a medical issue during the trip did not stop me either. Even though the hotel doctor transported me to the local Cabo hospital for some testing, I still attended the show at the cantina that evening on very little sleep. Your music just manages to give me multiple feelings, such as inspired, happy, or calm, depending on the song. It's hard to explain, but it just affects me in so many ways.

Therefore, I continue to request your music whenever I go through any further testing. I hope to be celebrating 10 years cancer free in October at the 75th Birthday Bash in Cabo.

The second part of my story was my trip to Cabo for your 70th Birthday Bash in 2017. Being recently single, I planned to just enjoy my independence, meet new people, and celebrate your birthday with fellow Redheads in attendance from the St. Louis area and all over. Unbeknownst to me at that time, another fellow Redhead (Matthew) travelled solo for the trip of a lifetime to see his favorite rocker at the cantina. Well, we met in the hotel lobby on October 14th while boarding the bus to the airport for our return to St. Louis. We stayed at the same resort for the entire week and never saw each other until that moment. Matthew and I had our first date several weeks afterwards when I contacted him first. We continued to date and get to know each other better over the next several months. Not only do we both share the same love for your music and you, but we also share the same birthday (December 6th). We have discovered that we share a lot of the same interests, such as fitness, travel, music, and personality characteristics. After previously being in long-term relationships, we both fell in love again with each other in that first year (I'll Fall In Love Again). Four years later, we are still together and going strong. I would have never guessed when I arrived in Cabo that I would find the one person in this world who is so compatible to me plus lived less than 30 miles from me on that trip. How often can someone say that? I can, and I believe it was fate and you that brought us together.

In conclusion, I sincerely want to say THANK YOU. My life has changed drastically, especially these last 4 years, for the better, and I believe I owe some of it to you. Looking forward to new music, meeting you again one day, possibly sharing a drink together, and the 75th birthday bash. Wishing you the best birthday ever and many more to come.

Lola Ann Whittaker, Redhead 'Til I'm Dead

By Daniel Greer

Weedsport NY I stood on top of a light pole base in the stands. Sammy said, "How's Weedsport? " Then pointed me out and said, "Hey man, that smells pretty good from here!" I held it in the air and the crowd went crazy. Then he said I'd like to party with all of you, but that would be kinda hard." But I tried.

When Eagles Fly

By Christopher Wheeler

It was in July 2002 when Owen, my two-year-old son, was diagnosed with

Medulloblastoma. It is a cancerous (malignant) brain tumor that starts in the lower back part of the brain. We lived in the suburbs of Atlanta and had to drive into the Scottish Rite Children's Hospital for doctor appointments, and overnight stays for chemo treatments.

Of course, me being a Redhead and Hagar fan from when I was a kid in the late '70s, I would listen to Sammy as we drove for Owen's treatments. Owen would love sitting in his car seat singing *Your love is driving me crazy*, with a big emphasis on "crazy,", shouting it out when we got to that point in the song. It was a rough road from the first day of Owen's diagnosis. When Sammy decided to go out on the road with David Lee Roth and head to Atlanta, I had to get tickets. Didn't care to see Roth at all, but Sammy didn't make it to Atlanta too often. I purchased one ticket in the front row. I couldn't wait. Sammy and his music have been such a big part of my life, from cruisin' the mall in high school, first kiss, to many other events in my life.

I have never been in front row for a concert, and this being my rock hero. I was driving everyone crazy about going, but being a father was even more important than going to see Sammy. And as with cancer, it throws many unexpected curves your way. The day of the concert, Owen woke up saying his head hurt and he had a high fever so we went to the hospital. Owen had to get a shunt, drainage tube, put into his brain to relieve buildup of fluid the cancer was causing. He was up and stable and doing well, but I could not leave him to go to the concert. He wanted daddy to stay with him that night, and I did. Sammy would just have to wait.

My wife Kim knew how much Sammy meant to me. No joke, Sammy to me is what John Lennon or Robert Plant is to others. His songs, his lyrics, his philosophy on life and love all falls into the way I was raised and what I believe. Sammy just provides that total connection to life for us.

Redheads. Not like the Beatle's craziness with girls fainting, but a connection on another level, a true respect. My wife knew how much it hurt not to be able to see Sammy that close, so she decided to see if she could contact Sammy's management to just get an autograph for me. Someone responded to her with a contact to a lady named Paula. Somehow Paula new someone or worked with Sammy. Kim told her the full story and Paula told her she would get something sent. It wasn't just an autograph. I got a package in the mail on the first of November. I opened it, and what was inside blew me away. It was a note saying: "Yo! Christopher and Owen, Check this out! PEACE" It was signed Sammy. Inside was a copy of the not-yet released *Not 4 Sale* cd, and he threw in a guitar pic as well. I was floored. And so it began, the new song we listened to as we went to treatments was the song *Not 4 Sale.* Now Owen would sit in his car seat singing: "All the money in the world". It was our little moment where we connected with Sammy.

By Thanksgiving that year Owen lost a lot of his speech due to the cancer and chemo. But he would still want to listen to Sammy and dance in his car seat His young body just couldn't take much more, and just shy of his third birthday, we lost Owen on New Year's Eve 2002. It was fast and hit me hard. Once again Sammy was there for me. *Eagles Fly* kept me going. I know this song was about being born and I kept telling myself my son was reborn in heaven, not in pain. I loved even though I had a short time on earth with Owen, he and I had a connection to each other that was Sammy Hagar.

Musings

By Danny Franco

I've only missed Sammy twice, once in Colorado, well my friends from high school excused me because, at a party, we listened to Sammy live on the radio from the Rainbow Music Hall. I've always seen him by accident, opening up for other bands, but what really set me off was the *3 Lockbox* tour. I was at that concert with a high school sweetie, which set the tone for spring break. I loved his stories that led into songs and saw how dedicated he his to his fans, holding up banners, slapping high-fives. I've been on a mission ever since to give Sammy a high five. Seeing him at Red Rocks was another highlight. I hope to meet him some day for a conversation, autograph, and a high-five.

By Darrin Carpenter

It was the summer of '83, and I just turned 16 with long road trip from Tulsa to San Diego with a large group. On the way back one day, I was tired of the tapes I had brought for my Walkman. I asked a girl if I could look through her tapes, and I not only discovered Three Lock Box, but Sammy that day. I proceeded to buy every Sammy cassette published Couldn't wait for VOA's release date! Got a ticket for the show in Tulsa in 1984. I. Was amazed at his great energy. When Sammy broke into Swept Away, running across the stage, I was a fan for life. Thanks for all the teen memories and beyond, Red Rocker. You've stayed true to who you are! Cheers!

By David McConnell

The first time I ever heard Sammy was when my best friend asked me to call KCAL and request the song *Red* by Sammy Hagar. The song rocked and I became a lifetime fan. My brother asked me what I wanted for my birthday and I requested a Sammy album. *All Night Long* was my first music and my brother asked who was singing and I said Sammy Hagar as I first played either *Bad Motor Scooter* or *Rock Candy.* Of course my brother exclaimed it was Montrose and I said it was Sammy. I didn't know who Montrose was. I have gone on to see Sammy more times than I can count in all his configurations from Sammy to Van Halen to Chickenfoot to the Wabos, to The Circle.

By David Myers

I've always been a Van Halen fan, and I always have been a Red Rocker fan. When Sammy became part of Van Halen, I became a big Van Halen fan. We would not miss a concert when they came to Wisconsin. Sammy was such a showman. I remember I was in the 14th row at Alpine Valley and I joked with my buddies you could see the white of Sammy's teeth So every time I think of Sammy, I think of those whitest teeth in rock and roll.

By Deborah McGrew

I have never gotten the chance to meet Sammy Hagar. I have absolutely loved him since I was a teenager, especially when Van Halen released *5150.* My walls were covered with pictures of Sammy and Michael Anthony. I am just a fan, I have been to numerous concerts. Sammy Hagar has been important in my life more than 40 years.

By Dee Granado Roark

Okay, we have to travel back in time to when my brother always listened to Sammy. I started getting interested after hearing some of his music and I've been hooked ever since. I began seeing his videos and he was different and that is a good different. My brother would let me borrow some music from time to time and here I am now, some 30 years later, still loving his music and concerts. He's an amazing singer and entertainer and always still my favorite until eternity. Thank You Red Rocker.

By Donna Bielecki

My Sammy intro was in the early '80s. I wanna say it was the *Three Lock Box* album,or *Standing Hampton*. Can't remember. I Just remember falling in love with that voice. Still love it. I even gave up senior prom to go to a Sammy concert. I remember the show at Cal Expo in Sacramento. I drank some Jack Daniel before going in, not smart, and went into the show and passed out, but woke up in time for Sammy. I moved to Spokane, Wash. in 1987. My first show there was Monsters of Rock at Joe Alibi Stadium. Awesome show as always. I remember Sammy's version of *Sitting on the Dock of the Bay*. Fast forward to 2019 my daughter bought me tickets to see Sammy at the Northern Quest Casino. My 7-year-old granddaughter begged me to take her. She came to me one day and said, "Grandma, I learned all the words to *I Can't Drive 55.* I did end up taking her a show in 2021 and watching her react to Sammy sing it was priceless.

Hot Poop

By Timm Johnson

I have thought long and hard on what my Sammy story would be.

The story of the first time I was close enough to talk to him, I walked into a two urinal restroom. I realized when he was washing his hands who he was. I was driving our '71 Cutlass with a Rocket 350 when I caught up to him on the highway. After flashing a peace sign, he showed me his car was faster.

The story of the next time I was close enough to speak with him was at the first Chickenfoot live concert that was held at El Corazon in Seattle. I was waiting at the back entrance holding our sons red JS 1200 guitar to get Joe to autograph it. How our son got our help purchasing the guitar is a story of its own. Sammy gets out of the limousine, happy as can be, and walks right up to me to autograph the guitar. I just had to look at him and say, "Sorry Sammy. I only have permission for Joe to sign it." He just smiled and kept going. Joe autographed the guitar saying, "What a lovely guitar."

The story about how I became a fan of the man is when my wife read the book "Red, My Uncensored Life in Rock" and told me of the similarities of our childhoods: abandoned by alcoholic fathers that were boxers but brought up by hard working mothers of strong faith. I learned that he is also a giver and shares his many blessings.

The Cabo Wabo in Cabo San Lucas, Mexico is our happy place in the world. Within moments of the first time I entered I knew this was an awesome place in the world. We decided to sit at the long metal bar in the concert area. Sitting ten feet away was a long haired Mexican gentleman. He looked at me and said, "You need a hair cut." Seeing how I only have long hair on the sides and am bald on top, I took off my hat and said, "I got one." We laughed and I knew right then I was in a place where I was comfortable.

Having returned several times since, I have never met an employee who is unhappy working there, or that has a negative thing to say about their bosses. Every one of them I have seen work hard and put off a positive vibe about how grateful they are for the work they have.

The story of our most recent trip to see Sammy was New Year's Eve 2022 and our travel to get there. We were scheduled to leave Walla Walla, WA on December 27th. Due to a snowstorm in the Pacific Northwest, we had to drive to Portland, OR, a 4 hour drive in good weather, get a hotel room, and fly out on the 28th. We were facing leaving our car in Portland for our vacation. We were bummed to say the least. We couldn't understand why SeaTac was not prepared for the storm. But they weren't. My 82 year old mother came up from Colorado for the Christmas holiday. She had to travel to Portland a few days after us. Because of the weather she was leery of driving the Columbia River Gorge. My brother who lives nearby was able to drive her to Portland and retrieve our car. Just made us think how everything happens for a reason. I kind of resemble Santa, it is what it is. In October as Sammy was leaving, I told him I would see him for New Year's. He said, "BS I need gifts MF."

New Year's Eve at Cabo Wabo was a night well spent. To begin we had a fantastic dinner with friends. I don't like tomato soup or juice but hope to duplicate the tomato bisque that was one of the dishes served. How the lobster was prepared for so many people so well is a mystery to me, and I love to prepare foods for hundreds of people at a time. After dinner, we went inside the concert area for the show. There was a bottle of Santo Blanco tequila and a bucket of beer. The house band is the best house band that my wife or I have ever had the pleasure to see on stage. The party was definitely on. When Sammy came out on stage, the energy in the room went to the next level. I walked up the stage, handed Sammy a red hat with the words "Hot Poop" on it, and as I handed the hat to him, said "Merry Christmas MF". I never know what I am going to say until it comes out and I could not believe that is what did. Sammy must have remembered what he said back in October, laughed, and wore the hat. Hot Poop is the oldest independently owned record store in the state of Washington. It is still owned and operated by the same great guy, Jim McGwinn. Once despised and now loved by our city officials. Sammy is great about autographing things for his fans and signed one that I gave to Jim. My wife, being a front row fanatic, was at the front of the stage while Sammy sang. One of the songs that he sang that night was "Can't Stop Loving You". While singing the song he held Teri's hand and even put the microphone down for her as she was singing along with him. That put her on a cloud and for the happiness that he gave her I am so thankful.

On January 5th we got to see Sammy honored as the first tourism ambassador of Los Cabos, Mexico. That evening he put on a free show like back in the old days of the Cabo Wabo. It was another outstanding day.

The travel home was exciting all on its own. We were passengers on a 737 800/900 headed to Seattle to transfer home. We had been in the air for around three hours when the pilot came over the intercom and informed the cabin that we were making an emergency landing in Fresno due to a fuel leak on the number 2 right side engine. Next, a flight attendant came over the intercom and said that there would be fire trucks waiting but it was standard procedure and there was no need for it to overly concern us. At that time, I am sure that people who haven't prayed in a while remembered how. The landing went text book. Not being an international airport, Fresno has no Customs department. We needed to wait on the tarmac over an hour for them to get there. Then we waited an hour for a different plane to be flown in from San Francisco. Then we had to go through U.S. security screening to get on the other plane. After boarding the other plane, we had to sit again another hour plus on the Tarmac for the original plane to be moved. Total delay time was over 4 hours so we missed our connecting flight. We got to Seattle and were told we couldn't get a flight home until 9:30 the next evening. We decided to rent a car. We were once again completely bummed about our delays but happy that we were alive. Leaving the airport, I stopped a security person next to an escalator to ask directions to the car rental agencies. While talking, a gentleman appearing to be in his 80's was getting on the escalator when he fell backwards going up on his back feet first. I was able to respond quickly enough that I was able to have the man standing ready to step off the escalator, a 14 second ride. Everything just seems to happen for a reason. Our delay going and our delay on our return, although at the time seemed to be a pain in the ass, turned out to be a blessing in disguise.

It is because of the positive environment that Sammy, Jorge, and Marco have created at the Cabo Wabo Cantina that is, to us, truly unparalleled in the hospitality industry that we were right there right then.We all live Right Now. Your next Right Now will start after this Right Now. Make it a joyful one.

Timm Johnson

By Doug Davis

I have a few stories. One being the 1980 Texas Jam. Sammy's *Ice Man* was his signature song. At the 1982 Texas Jam, he owned the show and we still talk about it. At the 2004 Houston Super Bowl, nobody knew Sammy was there. I stumbled into a tent and there he was. Then there was the VH reunion tour. We were given front-row seats by a couple walking out after the first song. Eddie was fucked up as a lab rat and Sammy was attempting to keep it rolling. Then I attended the show at the Woodlands and Sammy pulled a double show. Ithink the last time was Sugarland in 2017.

By Glenn Nicholson

In 1992, I saw Sammy in a Hartford, Conn; concert. It was the night before my real analysis exam at Eastern CT State University. I had a little guilt I should be studying instead of rocking it out. Sometimes in life you just say, "Fuck it". I still managed to get a B on the exam. The show was incredible. I love you guys and definitely missing Eddie.

By Gordon Watkins

More than 40 shows through the years. Sometimes three shows in three nights. Tahoe Wabo on opening night and every show, twice a year until the last. I saw the Wabos at Harrah's Rincon Casino. I heard them doing sound check behind the stage in the back lot where the show was going to be. Everybody got fired up. I wanted to see some warm-ups after the sound checks. I ordered another Red Rocker cocktail and went to my room to get ready. The elevator door was open when I walked up and there was Vic. We talked and later when I was at the show I saw Vic whisper in Sammy's ear and point at me. Sammy laughed while singing and gave me a thumbs up while pointing to Vic. Later Sammy's mom and sister were there and I waved them to a spot I had saved. Sammy, Vic, Mona and Bro all saw the commotion coming from where mom was and they were watching. Sammy figured out what had happened and, without missing a beat, he and Vic both came over; still playing and singing perfectly they both greeted the family and pointed at me with a thumbs up and a thank you. The show went on. I feel they all rocked it a little harder that night for mom.

By James Hatchett

Sammy climbing the scaffolding to damn near the top of the Astrodome during his encore song. That was early '80s at The Texas World Music Festival. I believe the year before he smashed a guitar and set it on fire. Also remember him, Ted Nugent, and Rik Emmet doing some Led Zeppelin. They were all at the show together.

By James Fowler

I first saw Sammy Hagar in '84 - the *VOA* tour. I have seen him a number of times since then. Cabo Wabo is always fun.

Musings

By Gregory Beehler

So here goes: Sammy is playing Glen Helen in California. We decide to go. It's my two kids, girl 12, boy 8, my wife, my dad, and his wife. They have a Van Halen tribute band on another stage which was super funny because the guy playing Dave was so over the top. So they have some classic cars out back, a bar, some tables and chairs, just super casual. It's probably 4 p.m. in the summer. My dad takes my son to go look at the cars while the rest of us are just sitting at a table with an umbrella while wearing these different colored Mexican straw hats they were giving away. Dad and son came back after 30 mins or so and says, "Hey, look what we got." They are each holding a ticket. Turns out one of Sam's guys was just walking around and saw my dad and son, struck up a conversation and hooked us up with third-row seats.

Shows about to start and my son and i put the wristbands on. Son is blown away; first real rock concert. After a few songs, I take him back to our seats and grab my daughter and bring her down for a few songs. Shows getting close to being over and I switch the kids out again. This time while my son and I are down there, the drunk females have decided it's time to take their bras off and throw them on stage. You know what comes next. So as cool as Sammy was, my kid never smiled so hard when he saw his first concert boob. Apparently, another guy saw my kids smile and said, "Concert boobs are cool right?" Kid says yes.

By James Kellum

VH1 had a Sammy Hagar contest about why you are a fan. I sent them a video and I won the contest but they wanted to surprise me so they told my wife and I came home and my house was turned into a little Cabo Wabo and I was on TV. was there with his latest CD *Not for Sale*. We did some shots of Cabo Wabo tequila. Sammy brought three bottles.

By Jay Hotrum

I first saw Sammy open for Black Sabbath, Van Halen and Boston at Anaheim stadium in California 1979 and was hooked. Followed him everywhere like all of us Redheads do now. Then a local radio station in Los Angeles (KMET) had an April Fools Day party and a contest where the winner met Sammy during the Three Lock Box tour at the Forum in LA. I made a shirt that said "ET, The Extra Testicle" and wore shorts with balloons coming out of them. I won the contest and met Cheech Marin, who took photos with me, then he later stole the bit and used it in one of the Cheech and Chong movies. It became pop history. The night of the show I was picked up in a limo, driven to the Forum and brought into the Lakers' dressing room. Sammy came in gave me T-shirts, an autographed Three Lock Box record, and we took photos with radio station personalities. We got front-row lodge tickets During the show, suddenly the lights in the place went dark. It was pitch black, a spotlight came on from the stage and started spinning around, just one light everyone watching and it stopped on me. I stood up on the rails in front of me, threw my hands in the air and started yelling: "wooooo hooo." The entire audience was watching me and the lights came on all at once and it was Sammy holding the spotlight pointing at me, laughing his head off.

By Jim Kuzminsky

When I was 17-years-old, I worked at the racetrack at Cal Expo in Sacramento I had a pass to get into the grandstands where Sammy was performing. I watched the warm-up, climbed the scaffolding, and me and my brother-in-law were two of the only people in the grandstands because it was early afternoon. Most of the show I don't remember because I was hammered. After the show, while they were tearing down, I tried to talk one of his roadies into letting me become a roadie. It might've worked out for me if I hadn't been so hammered, but I had a good time. I've seen Sammy several times since then. Thankfully, not so hammered. Long live the Red Rocker. Thanks for the memories, Sammy. RIP Eddie Van Halen.

By John Dettore

I was living in Vegas in 1999 and the KOMP radio station had a contest for a meet n greet before Sammy's show. I won. The show was July 3, three days before my birthday and I got to meet Sammy. He was the nicest, coolest guy and I was so excited I got to meet the Red Rocker. I've seen Sammy live 25 times. Keep on rocking, Sammy, and I love my baby poundcake. Thank you for all the years of the greatest tunes on earth.

By John Jahn

My first boat was named "Cabo Wabo." I got to high-five him at the Pontiac Silverdome after a Pistons' game and before the Monsters of Rock. I proposed to my wife with, *Don't Make Me Wait.* At my wedding, the mother-son dance was "Child to Man." I attended the 70th Birthday Bash and I am on the video. I have the *Don't Make Me Wait*' lyrics as a wedding gift that I would love to get autographed.

By FF John Sepa Retired E-38 Bronx N.Y.

Sammy threw a private thank you concert for first responders after 9/11 at Irving Plaza in New York City NYC. Free Cabo Wabo tequila and more than 500 people. Great show with loud in your face rock and roll and the perfect medicine at the right time for fireman, cops, and EMT's that really needed someone. Sammy, to give us an opportunity to get hammered and rock out... forever grateful.

By Judah Tate

My first Sammy show was in 2021. My "memo" forced me to listen to Sammy since I was baby. I wore a shirt to the show that said "My memo made me come." I enjoyed the show and rocked out. I realized Sammy's not too bad. See ya soon. Happy Birthday.

Musings

By Katelyn Taylor

My first show was in 2021. I have been listening to Sammy since birth. My mamaw listens to him and so do we. I want to go to Cabo with my mamaw. I liked my first show and I'm ready to see Sammy again. Happy birthday

By Kathy O'Conner

I still remember going to Cabo for the first time in 1996 and walking into the Cabo Wabo to hear Sammy sing on his birthday. I have been going back to Cabo ever since for the Birthday Bash. I miss the fun times waiting in line to get a wristband and meeting other Redheads I have remained friends with. I have lost track how many times I have seen Sammy in concert. I have been to his concerts in Lake Tahoe, Concord, Dixon May Fair, Sacramento and more. Sammy really gives back to his fans and is always ready to provide an autograph or a picture. I also cherish my friendships with his adult children.

By Kelly Baker

Sammy is such a great person. Met him in Memphis and have been to many shows with more planned. My last experience was the beach bar promo on the Las Vegas strip. Hopped on a plane and shared a room with a West Coast Redhead. We waited all day for the band to show up. We were VIP behind the band because they faced the strip It was a great sing-a-long. Kari was standing beside the stage with their dog. It was a fast trip but worth every second!

By Kenneth Carpentier

I've got to be the biggest Redhead. Someone broke into my house and stole all my records and all my ticket stubs. I had every Sammy Hagar album. I'm lost. Thank you, Sammy, for letting me grow up with you.

By Matt Booher

I was a huge Boston fan, they came to Oklahoma in 1978. I was in eighth grade and my older brother promised me a ticket if I'd wash his car. The day of the show I asked for the ticket and he didn't have one for me. About an hour later he showed up with a restricted view ticket for me. I was bummed I wouldn't see everything, but ecstatic I was going. He told me Sammy

Hagar was opening and I had no idea who he was. He told me Sammy had been the lead singer for Montrose. Ok, didn't know them either. We got to the venue. Sammy came out and rocked our asses off. My only real memory of him from that show is him sitting on the front of the stage with the lap guitar doing *Bad Motor Scooter.* I've been a fan ever since. Sadly, I haven't had the opportunity to meet Sammy although. I've seen him every time he's played in Oklahoma except once.

Musings

By Mary Tucknott

I attended my first concert back in in the late '90s in Illinois. The man I was dating got us backstage passes through a contest. It was the best time I have ever had. We danced, drank, and partied on the stage. I even got to dance with Sammy on the stage. I would love to do that again. PLEASE.

By Matt Bywater

We're going back to 1980, maybe 1979. I'm a huge Hagar fan. I was born and raised in Fremont, Calif. My brother turned me on to Sammy with the *Musical Chairs* album, and I was hooked. Sammy's voice blew me away. I've seen him live at least 15 times in concert. I wanted to meet him somehow, so me and a buddy of mine found out what town he lived in. We drove there where we saw a cab, and asked the driver if he knew where Sammy Hagar lived. He pulled out a map and we followed him to Sammy's house. In the driveway was a Ferrari BB512, the car used in the *I can't drive 55* video and a BMW 635. We were nervous and didn't want to seem rude or anything, but we knocked on the door and Betsy opened the door We asked, "Is Sammy home? We are big fans and just want to tell him we love his music. She came back with two signed pictures of him and said he couldn't come to the door. We thanked her. As we walked down the driveway to leave, we saw a black trash bag that looked like clothes were in it. We grabbed the bag and threw it in my truck. In that bag was a nice dress made in Italy, a red wind breaker with the name Aaron written on the tag inside, and some invoices from Capital records. Went back to his house and left some Heineken beer and a birthday card.

By Matt Moffitt

I've been fortunate to meet Sammy several times. First time took place in 1991 in Indianapolis. I happened to have front row seats to Van Halen. I was only 18, met Sammy and the band the day before. He couldn't have been any nicer. Hearing a nervous 18-year-old, asking rapid-fire questions, and then, somehow, I got a backstage pass to the next nights VH show. Sammy met with me, my friend, and a few others. He He made us margaritas. Asked if I was 21 *wink wink*. I said, "Yes". I still have the triple sec bottle from that night!! I also got to hang out with him backstage a few other times . Me and a friend ordered him 44 red balloons on his birthday to his hotel room in Philly. I bet he remembers that one.

By Nikki Anderson

My first Sammy show the Texas Jamm 1980. I have been listening to Sammy since in the womb. My mom was pregnant with me at the Jamm. I have been to several r shows with my mom. We played Chickenfoot at my dad's celebration of life. I was blessed to have rocking parents, who taught us to feel music. I can't wait for more. Ready to rock!! I hope Sammy has blessed and happy birthday.

Musings

By Matt Talluto

It was on the *Marching to Mars* tour, I was hosting the afternoon show for 98.9 The Bear in Fort Wayne, Ind. After escorting listeners backstage to meet Sammy, my wife and I found ourselves back there with Sammy and his wife after everyone had cleared out. Our wives had their own conversation going and, as much as I was flipping in my head due to being a Van Halen freak, there I was hanging with Sammy. I was telling him how we were planning a trip to Cabo. He asked if we were going to his club while there.Of course we were and Sammy told us to ask for Jorge. When we arrived in Cabo, we took a shuttle from our resort to Cabo Wabo for a late lunch. My wife reminded me to ask for Jorge. Soon a guy with long black hair, and dressed in black leather said, "Welcome to Cabo Wabo". I told him I worked in radio and met Sammy backstage earlier in the year. Believe it or not he had my name on a list and he gave us a tour and everything was on the house. Thank you, Sammy (and Jorge), for creating such a great memory.

By Pete Gilbertson

It was 1986 and the first concert with Sammy singing with Van Halen at the Hirsch Coliseum in Shreveport, LA. I was in the U.S. Air Force, stationed in Louisiana. I had to borrow a car to go to the show and, being a general admission show, I did not want to be late. As with most plans that did not work out, I arrived and parked as the doors were about to open. To my surprise, not one person was in line towards the back of thebuilding and when the doors opened, I walked in. I was able to go to the front of the stage; center left. Bachman Turner Overdrive opened and really got the place rocking. As they left the show, the fans on the floor started pushing closer to the stage. The barricade didn't prevent from people crushing towards the front and pleadings from the stage for people to stop pushing did not work. All of a sudden, the barricade snapped and fell over, tossing people into the stage headfirst. It got quiet. The security team made sure everyone was ok. I did not see anyone get hurt but everyone that fell forward was moved to the right side of the stage. It was announced if everyone did not move back, they would cancel the show. Slowly the fans moved back and the security team, along with the roadies, repaired he barricade. This is where I got lucky. I never had to move and when they let everyone move closer to the stage, I was center stage, directly under Sammy's mic. When Van Halen came out, Sammy gave me and a couple other guys a high- five and the show took off. It was an amazing performance. Looking back, the funny part of the whole situation was that Sammy sang the show with his headset mic and was never really center stage, running all over, and even up into the rigging above the stage when he sang *Ain't Talking Bout Love*.

By Paul Mendoza

Back in the day, we went to see REO Speedwagon. It was Joe Cocker, REO, and Bebop deluxe. REO cancelled and Sammy opened. Right out of Montrose, Sammy put on the best show I have seen to this day. Bebop played two songs and were booed off the stage. Joe hurled twice in the first two songs. Although he managed to finish, we left early with the sound of *Bad Motor Scooter* still ringing in our ears.

Musings

By Rhonda Valluzzi

I first saw Sammy Hagar open up for Boston in Las Vegas somewhere, in the late '70s. I was amazed at this guy climbing all over walls with cars in the backdrop. After that, I moved to Chicago and saw Sammy play everywhere. One year, I had front-row tickets at Tinley Park, and he invited us all to his birthday party in Cabo. My husband and I went and I met the most wonderful Redheads. We've followed Sammy to shows in Minnesota, Wisconsin, Florida, Indiana and Saint Louis. The best times were when people were able to go on stage. He was playing in Tampa, we had stage passes. Sammy just snatched me and my cousin up and was singing to us. I also saw Sammy at the Super Bowl in 2004. It was the best three shows, in a row, of my life. Sammy wrote the songs of my life and I had the best time traveling with my hubby. I will cherish these memories for ever.

By Ron Moore

In 1981, I was 18 years old and attended a concert at The Country Club in Reseda, Calif. The headliner was Gamma, Ronnie Montrose's band at the time. I had been a Montrose fan since 1976 and an aspiring guitarist. Right after the Gamma show, I talked my way backstage, telling security I just wanted to meet and speak to Ronnie for a college journalism project. When I got backstage, I saw a large group of people gathered around a table with everyone smiling and having a good time. I walked closer to the group of people and suddenly, I was standing face-to-face with Sammy Hagar. I'm sure I looked surprised and dumbfounded. Before I could get any words out, Sammy patted me on my shoulder like he knew me and asked how it was going. He was the friendliest rock star I ever met.

By Ryan Hoyle

My first-time seeing Sammy as a solo act was in San Jose at a small festival at the fairgrounds n the late '90s. I went to see Sevendust and Megadeth. Sammy was the headliner. It was a great concert, then Sammy came out and it became a great party. The best I can explain it is that it felt like Sammy was there to have a good time and we were there to party with him. I liked Sammy before, but at that point I was hooked. I've seen his concerts as often as I could ever since.

By Scott Bartlett

I was a huge Montrose fan, but Sammy was gone, moved on. I heard he was playing at this old movie theater turned into a rock club in Milwaukee. No one else could go, but I had to do it by myself. I got the table by the railing on the bar level. Great seat. Sammy came out and sat down on the edge of the stage with that steel guitar kind of thing on his lap and just tore into *Bad Motor Scooter* for the first song. I knew I made the right choice that evening.

Musings

By Scotty Ford

I'm one of the many of the behind-the-scenes characters involved with keeping Sammy out doing shows. I have driven the forklift at the warehouse, as well as loading and unloading the tour truck when it departs and arrives back to the compound. I don't look at it as a job as much as I look at it as fun. I have been the man on the lift for the last five years. I will be reporting tomorrow to unload a truck returning from Texas.

By Peter Stass

My wife Jill and I have been to many concerts through the years. The first arena show we went to was Van Halen at the Skydome in Toronto in 1991. She was meant to be going to see Les Miserables with her friends, but luckily, she picked Van Halen with me. Love you baby. We will be celebrating our 30th Wedding anniversary on Oct. 3rd, 2022.

Editor Shelley Shepherd-Klaner's story in pictures. First Montrose story after Ronnie recovered from cancer. Produced Montrose Wabos Show. Promoted Ronnie Montrose Remembered. Published stories about Chickenfoot, Sammy. Photo of Sammy & Shelley in county paper for rum bash.

By Sherri Graflage

I saw Sammy every time he came to St. Louis for more than 30 years. He never disappoints. The most memorable time was Superjam at Busch Stadium in his red trans am. Until, that is, when I went to his Birthday Bash in Cabo. I don't think I will ever top that, but I will try.

By Tiffany Askren

In 1999, my dad took me to my first concert, Rockfest, and Sammy Hagar headlined. I was raised on rock and roll, but Sammy helped mold my love for the genre. When he sang Lay Your Hand On Me, I was in a trance. My dad and I sang and danced. It built our relationship and my love for music. I'll always have Sammy to thank for that. He tours and plays music and I'm not sure if he ever truly knows or realizes the impact he has on people. I was 11-years-old and I could not even tell you who else played at that event, but because of Sammy, I will always remember my first concert with my dad.

By Tom Barnes

Back in the early '90s, I won an MTV contest to go to the grand opening of Cabo Wabo Cantina. I met the whole band and got to hang out with them for a while. I brought one of my guitars with me and Eddie Van Halen signed it for me. I still have it. Sammy was the coolest guys I've ever met, just 5 minutes of him being a good guy, to me, lasted a lifetime as an awesome memory. Keep rocking Sammy.

By Arthur Curry

In El Paso, Texas on Father's Day, at Speaking Rock Casino, Sammy rocked the roof off. I have seen Sammy in Texas, Arizona, and New Mexico with the Cabos, Van Halen, solo, and Chickenfoot. I have been following Sammy for a very long time and will continue to follow him as long as he plays.

Sammy Story –
By Donna Murphree

February 14, 2022

It all started at Rocklahoma, 1980 – a rock festival with Van Halen as the headline band. I had just turned 15 and worked my first job over the summer to earn cash to fund my music and concert addiction. I bought tickets to see Van Halen with my own money that I had earned! I was so excited and proud! My best friend in high school was a year older, so she drove us to the concert in Norman which was at the Oklahoma Sooners football stadium. Sammy was up first. I had never heard of him at the time, nor do I remember any of the songs he sang specifically that day. What I do remember is watching him take the stage, dressed in red, shredding his cool guitar. His hair was long, blond, and curly, oh my! I know now that he was much older than I thought at the time. He looked to be in his early 20's and this girl wanted to get a closer look! I tried to talk my friend into going to the front, but she didn't want to risk losing her spot. I couldn't stand it and started making my way to the stage. There was a crowd right at the front that did not want to let me in. I got shoved, screamed at, and elbowed in the head – it was brutal. All the while promising everyone that I pushed in front of that it was only for a minute! Then it happened, I was as close as I could get to the stage as he started transitioning into the next song when our eyes connected, and he smiled big and winked at ME! Can I say, HOLY SHIT? I was HOOKED! I thought I had just found my one true love, lol! Good thing I had that job because I was just about to spend a small fortune on albums, t-shirts, posters, and music magazines. I bought every Sammy thing I could get my hands on. My entire bedroom was COVERED with Sammy posters and memorabilia.

My teenage years were traumatic and music was my escape. Sammy Hagar was THE one for me. I literally think if I wouldn't have had the comfort of his music and the distraction of crushing on him, I might not have had the strength to make it. He became my best friend that I had never met. Rocklahoma was the only time in my teenage years that I would get to see him live. I'm not sure he ever came back to Oklahoma as a solo artist and, by the time he joined Van Halen, I was out of school, and married with a baby. Life, at that time, didn't afford me the luxury of going to concerts. I still kept up with his music and his life though. I remember rocking my baby, watching MTV for hours, waiting for one of his music videos to come on.

Fast forward to 2020. Life punched me in the face. I experienced some of the most hurtful and grievous things a person can go through. I was in a very sad and dark place. One day, as I was sitting on my porch crying and asking God to help me find a way through my situation, I thought of my youth and the rough things I went through at that time. Then I remembered Sammy. I decided I was going to pull out those records and start listening again. I started listening to Space Between and began to heal. It's as if we were on the same life journey, dealing with adult stuff now, not teenage angst. We were growing older together. Recently, in my iPhone notes, I found a file where I wrote the following: "COSMIC 1980 REPEAT!! Affirmation is speaking to me on a SPIRITUAL level! Been on repeat for hours – blowing my mind!" It's the same soul connection I felt with Sammy's music when I was a teenager. His new stuff is connecting with me DEEPLY.

I started looking to see if he was touring. I needed to see him live again. I found out that he was coming to Oklahoma in September 2021 and quickly purchased my tickets. At the same time, I came up with an idea to make a timeline poster of music memories of Sammy Hagar and I was going to have him sign it. I came up with a design and drew it out on piece of poster board, then a friend, who is a talented artist, turned it into a masterpiece! I told my husband and friends that Sammy was going to sign my poster and they laughed at me. They said, "Don't get your hopes up!" and "I can't imagine you getting close enough to Sammy to get him to sign your poster!" But I knew. I felt it. We ended up on the second row in Durant, Oklahoma at a beautiful new casino venue and I had my awesome poster in a tube, ready to hand to him. That night, we weren't allowed to stand against the stage. The concert started and I was in HEAVEN! It had been 40 years since I saw him live. I literally had goosebumps all over my body. The second he approached stage left, I grabbed my poster tube and ran up and handed it to him. He was just beginning a song and before he started singing, he said, "I know you!" and smiled and took the tube. WTF?! He had to have me confused with someone else or something. I had no idea. But it made me giddy!! He took the tube with my poster and sat it on the stage. I waited and waited for him to pick it up. Every time he would come back to stage left, I ran up and said, "Sign my poster!" Finally, the third time, he said, "I WILL!" and laughed at me. He took it and put it on the drum riser. YESSSSSSS!! I knew it! He is going to sign my poster!! Towards the end of the concert, he pulled the poster out and showed the audience and signed it! Mikey even signed it too!! Then when he came over and handed it back to me, he was singing "Your Love is Driving me Crazy" and he stood and sang it directly to ME for what felt like a lifetime. BOOM – Sammy saved my life again! He had no idea how God used him to begin to heal my heart. I will cherish that memory forever. I'm actually weeping as I'm writing this now.

Well, the story doesn't end there. That Durant concert was the beginning of my Sammy spree. I continued to go to concert after concert until I wrapped up 2021 with 10 shows under my belt! At the Strat shows in Vegas in November, I was finally able to meet him during a VIP event before one of the shows. For days, I had practiced what I was going to tell him. Then, when he walked in the room and I was approaching him, I felt myself start to cry. So, to avoid crying, I grabbed him and hugged him tight. I know he thought I was just a crazy fan girl, but I'm just SO GRATEFUL for him. It's the only thing I could do. I couldn't talk to him without getting emotional, so I thought to ask him to sign my ankle above my '55' tattoo and he DID! Then, he hugged me again. It was the most perfect night. I flew back to Oklahoma with my head in the clouds and went straight to the tattoo shop to make it permanent.

The last year has been such a blessing! With Affirmation on repeat, I believe I manifested all those lyrics. MAKE FRIENDS! Because of Sammy I have met so many great people and many of them have become close friends. Redheads are the coolest cats on the planet, and they feel like family. BELIEVE! I believed I would get my poster signed! It is something I'll cherish from now on. LOVE! I love Sammy Hagar and want him to know that he is much more than entertainment. He is a life force that continues to keep this girl's ship from sinking. Thank you for everything, Sammy. You ROCK!

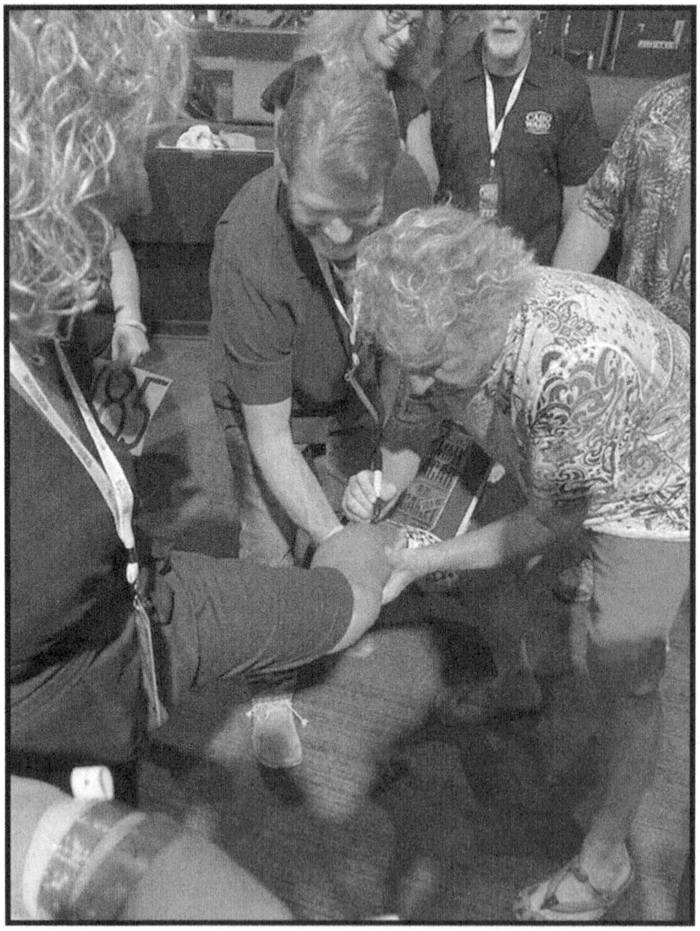

Special Guitar Finally Signed

By Dale Jarvis

I bought a special guitar back in 2000 and had been wanting to get it signed ever since. My wife and I had tickets for both the June 1st and 2nd 2019 concerts in St. Augustine, Florida and decided on a whim that we would take it down with us in hopes that we might magically run into Sammy being we had two full days there. As fate would have it, who do I run into in the lobby but Sammy himself! He was on the move but said hello and asked if I was going to the show. I told him we would be at both shows and he gave me a thumbs up and said awesome. We went to the concert (which of course was great) with the plans of getting back in time to maybe catch Sammy returning to the hotel. We did in fact see him and his wife and pup as well as the rest of the band but we could tell they were tired and in a rush to get upstairs and so I didn't want to bother him with the guitar. They did say hello to the small group of fans that were in the lobby which was nice. The next day we ended up running into Sammy's manager Wayne at the hotel bar and told him about my guitar and how badly I wanted to get it signed. He told us he would call up and let Sammy know there was a small group of fans that wanted to get a couple of things signed to see if he would be willing to do so on his way out to the show. It appeared he was so I ran up and got my guitar and came back down to the lobby. A few minutes later Kari and Money walked out followed by Sammy. He was very genuine and said hello to all of us and shook all of our hands. He took a few selfies with a couple of fans and then looked at my guitar and said "You want me to sign that thing or what"? He also commented on it saying it was the "real deal". My wife filmed the whole encounter and we were able to get a picture with him as well. It was an incredible experience and I couldn't have asked for a more perfect meeting. I was able to take my guitar back up to the room and then roll out to that night's concert on cloud 9.

Sammy Peed in my Bucket

By Shellie Keylon

Where do I even begin?

It was 1981. The movie *Heavy Metal* with the title song by Sammy was released. My boyfriend, myself and brother, all went to the drive-in theater to see it. In all honesty, I didn't watch much of the movie, but when the song came on, I was thoroughly blown away. I had no idea who was singing, but i knew I had to find out, which of course, I did.

Was hooked ever since. I must've listened to that song more than 30 times a day. Drove my foster parents nuts. Not like I didn't listen to other music, but from Sammy, it was just that one song. Eventually, I did listen to more than just that one song.

In 1984, my sister, who was 14, was dating a guy a couple years older than me. He was a huge fan and introduced me to *3 Lock Box*. I was totally mesmerized. I didn't immediately know it was Sammy but I soon put two and two together.

The boyfriend became handy because he then introduced me to Montrose. *Rock Candy* became another tune on speed dial and by the time *I Can't Drive 55* came out, my mission begun – to see Sammy live.

Fast forward to 2021. My niece and I planned a girls trip to Oklahoma to go to a museum. It just happened Sammy was playing at The River Spirit Casino. It was fate...destiny...kismet... I told my niece that this was meant to be. We booked a hotel room, reserved a rental car, and went online and found front-row tickets. I bought two tickets, but my niece was not interested so I ended up going with Donna Murphree, who has now become my soul sister.

I met Donna and her husband, Kreg, at the casino with tickets in hand. We hit it off like we had known each other for years. After waiting what seemed like forever, we were in.

After waiting 40 years to see Sammy I wanted him to autograph something special. Since it was on my bucket list, I brought a bucket to fill with Sammy souvenirs. Kreg decorated the bucket. I went up by the stage with my bucket in hand and Sammy autographed it after pretending to act like he was peeing in it. During the show I got fist bumps, some hand grabbings and other special memories. The trip to Oklahoma will always be one of my prized experiences.

Donna told me she was going to be attending the recent Las Vegas Residency shows. I found available tickets on a date they did not have tickets for and offered them to my friends and Kreg was unable to go, so I ended up being Donna's date.

She told me that she also had a surprise for me and we had to be in Vegas on Thursday instead of Friday. Turns out we would have another party pit show.

I feel extremely lucky to have had this experience. Redheads are an extremely wonderful group of people. I remain in touch with several of them and cannot wait to see them again. Thanks to Sammy for the wonderful years of music and performances. Thank you for making this midwestern farm girls dream come true. I decided to make this book a reality for Sammy's birthday as a way of saying thank you.

Thank You!

We would like to thank the following people and companies for their help and donations in being able to create this book. Without you, this would not have been possible.

Adam Kanning

Brett Carroll

Chris Packey

Donna Bristow

Felicia Urioste

Jeff Forrester

Lauren Vercruysse

Timm and Teri Johnson

Tommy Gerbic (BajaToms)

Shelley Shepherd-Klaner

And to the entire Redhead family that participated in contributing their stories. Thank you so much.

About the Creator of this work

Michelle Keylon was born in Wichita, Kansas. Raised in small town USA, Trimble, Mo. she became a Sammy fan in the early '80s. She wanted to do something special for Sammy's 75th birthday and "what better way than to have others join me in telling him how much he means to us? How much his music has helped some of us through various times of our lives? I created this to celebrate a special, kind, and giving human being that has brought me so much happiness."

About the Editor

Shelley Shepherd-Klaner hails from the Cleveland, Ohio area, where she got her feet early on, first as an Osmond fan, then experiencing the '70s, which she writes about in her book Step in Time with stories about Kent State, drug use, racial divide and more, sharing the landscape of the time to lyrics from Van Halen and Led Zeppelin and other bands. She graduated from Brigham Young University in Provo, Utah with a double major in Communications with an emphasis in print journalism and Psychology. She worked at Osmond Publishing and the BYU Press, as well as a reporter for the Provo Daily Herald and the BYU Daily Universe in the 1980s. She later moved to California, where she worked as an editor, reporter and publisher for 30 years. A New York Times newspaper made her an entertainment reporter, where she got her feet wet writing about Montrose, Todd Rundgren, Santana, Jefferson Airplane and other bands for eight years. She later wrote for *Rock World Magazine* out of Los Angeles, covering Evanescence, Chickenfoot, Sammy Hagar and more. She then became the music editor for a San Francisco website. Her work in the music industry created relationships with many artists and she worked on the promotion of the first Ronnie Montrose Remembered concert at NAMM after his death. She also promoted Scott Weiland's last album before his passing. She is a popular radio star reviewing and promoting many acts in California. She earned her master's degree in humanities with an emphasis in creative writing from Dominican University in San Rafael, Calif.

Cover art by Tommy Gerbic

Made in the USA
Middletown, DE
30 December 2022

20641973R00044